AF173834

THE PASSIVE INCOME MILLIONAIRE

LEARN HOW TO MAKE MONEY ONLINE, INVEST IN STOCKS, QUIT YOUR JOB, AND HAVE AN EARLY RETIREMENT

ALEXUS ARELLANO

Copyright © 2020 Alexus Arellano

All rights reserved.

TABLE OF CONTENTS

Copyright 2020 By Alexus Arellano - All rights reserved.

The following Book is reproduced below with the goal of providing information that is as accurate and reliable as possible. Regardless, purchasing this eBook can be seen as consent to the fact that both the publisher and the author of this book are in no way experts on the topics discussed within and that any recommendations or suggestions that are made herein are for entertainment purposes only. Professionals should be consulted as needed prior to undertaking any of the action endorsed herein.

This declaration is deemed fair and valid by both the American Bar Association and the Committee of Publishers Association and is legally binding throughout the United States.

Furthermore, the transmission, duplication or reproduction of any of the following work including specific information will be considered an illegal act irrespective of if it is done electronically or in print. This extends to creating a secondary or tertiary copy of the work or a recorded copy and is only allowed with express written consent from the Publisher. All additional right reserved.

The information in the following pages is broadly considered to be a truthful and accurate account of facts and as such any inattention, use or misuse of the information in question by the reader will render any resulting actions solely under their purview. There are no scenarios in which the publisher or the original author of this work can be in any fashion deemed liable for any hardship or damages that may befall them after undertaking information described herein.

Additionally, the information in the following pages is intended only for informational purposes and should thus be thought of as universal. As befitting its nature, it is presented without assurance regarding its prolonged validity or interim quality. Trademarks that are mentioned are done without written consent and can in no way be considered an endorsement from the trademark holder.

INTRODUCTION

Before we get into the different types of passive income, let's first talk about what it actually is. Passive income is money that is earned from a source in which he or she is not physically involved. Like active income, passive income is taxed, though it is usually treated a little differently by the Internal Revenue Service (IRS). States differ slightly in their tax laws, so make sure to see a certified public accountant before filing your taxes with the IRS.

Overall, there are three types of income. Passive, which is the subject of this e-book, active and portfolio income. To give a little insight into the difference between the three, we will briefly outline active and portfolio income before delving into different types of passive income.

Although it should seem self-explanatory, we are going to detail what active income is. Active income is a job that requires the earner to be physically present. In the United States, the most common forms of active income are hourly and salary. Hourly employees earn a wage for each hour they work while salary employees are paid a flat rate regardless of how many hours they put in. Most companies pay weekly or biweekly, although there are a few who pay monthly. However, those tend to be government or teaching positions.

Surprisingly enough, freelance work is also considered active income. The person in the freelance position gets paid for work upon its completion. One of the downfalls of freelance work is if you are sick or unable to complete a project, there is no paycheck. Writing articles, e-books and traditional books and photography are the most common types of freelance jobs.

Portfolio income is money earned from royalties, investments, capital gains and dividends. For tax purposes, the IRS does not consider portfolio income to be passive income as it does not come from traditional businesses or passive investments.

Now that we have talked about the different types of income let's talk about why passive income is a great way to earn extra money for savings, retirement, vacations or anything else you would like to spend your money on.

While you should be very excited about what we will learn in this book, it is important to note that passive income does not mean 'easy money.' Like all other forms of income, there is some work involved whether it is research, development, writing an e-book or selling photographs online. Wouldn't turning a hobby into income be an excellent way to earn some extra money? One of the ways we will discuss in this book is exactly that. Even using a hobby to earn a passive income takes some time and effort up front, although it is probably the most enjoyable of all the forms of passive income, we will cover in this book.

If you have some time and energy to devote to passive income from the comfort of your own home (maybe even in your pajamas while you sip coffee), let's talk about some of the exciting ways you can earn a passive income!

Chapter 1

Surveys, Selling Photos

& Teaching Classes

Surprisingly enough, there are lots of ways to make money on the internet. We will list some of the more passive ways to earn money online and then give you some insight into how you can get going with passive income online.

Websites like InboxDollars actually pay people to shop online, play games and even search the web. InboxDollars has been around since 2000, and the company itself employs thirty people. They offer anywhere between 1-10 cents per email read and the payment on playing games or going to an affiliate website varies. As with any web-based income potential, there are pros and cons to InboxDollars. The first payment isn't sent until you've earned thirty bucks. At that, it can take up to two weeks to receive payment so if you are looking for quick and easy, InboxDollars isn't the place to be. However, if you are hanging out in front of a computer while sipping on a latte at your local coffee shop, why not sign up and earn some money simply for surfing the net or reading emails? You are already online anyway, right?

Another site similar to InboxDollars is called **SwagBucks.** InboxDollars website is a little easier to maneuver, and they categorize each option for earning cash online. SwagBucks does require you to sign up with them before you can see the earning potential. Swagbucks doesn't pay in cold, hard cash. They pay in the form of "SwagBucks," which is their term for earning points. Each SwagBuck is approximately one cent. That means once you've accrued one-hundred, you've made roughly one dollar. SwagBucks are redeemable for gift cards only. There are no checks or payments sent to your PayPal account. As opposed to InboxDollars, SwagBucks will actually pay you for referrals, in the form of their SwagBucks, of course. For every survey your referral completes, you get ten percent. That's actually a great deal considering it is someone else doing the work, right? One last thing to mention about these websites. They both pay you to sign up for trial offers, which is something you need to be very careful with. While they both will pay a pretty decent amount for your signing up, you have to remember to cancel your membership within the month, or your credit card will be charged for the service. Of the two, Swagbucks pays more; usually enough to earn a twenty-five dollar gift card, which is actually a fantastic deal!

In addition to earning a passive income by signing up for websites like those mentioned previously, you can also sell your photography online. Obviously, this is geared toward those who enjoy taking photos as a hobby. As it isn't for everyone, we will discuss it briefly before moving onto the next subject.

If you do enjoy taking photos of scenic overlooks, nature, or even people (with their permission of course), you can sell your photos to places like Shutterstock and Stock photo. Depending on which site you choose, they will pay either with a percentage of overall sales of your photo or a flat fee for each photo that is sold to the client. One of the great things about selling your photos is one picture can earn money more than once. Each time it is sold, you'll get a percentage (or the aforementioned flat fee). If you always liked photography but hadn't really given it a second thought, maybe now is the time to do so. You do have to go out and take the pictures, but it is a great way to get some exercise, fresh air, see some awesome sights and earning some of that passive income!

Another way to earn passive income is to write an e-book. Like photography, it has to be something that you have an interest in. Since it isn't everyone's cup of tea, we'll go over it briefly, just like we did with photography.

There are several ways to make money with writing e-books. Fiction, fantasy, how-to, cookbooks...the list is endless. There is some work up front, and if you aren't the best with commas and periods, it might be prudent to hire an editor just to make sure you don't miss anything major. Some of the most popular books are how to and fantasy. If you are particularly knowledgeable on a subject, or you have an incredibly active imagination, either of those would be an excellent way to start earning passive income.

Once the book is written, you can publish it on Amazon and wait for some money to start coming in. If you want to make decent money, you will want to invest some time in marketing. This is something you can do yourself using your already established social media outlets. Facebook, Twitter, and Instagram are great for free advertising.

Did you know that you can make money by posting YouTube videos online? This too takes some work and a bit of marketing on your part, but once you get going who knows? Maybe you will be the next YouTube sensation! As we outlined with writing an e-book, there are several areas in which you can create a YouTube channel. Book or restaurant reviews, music, opinions, comedy, music and tutorials of all kinds including hair, makeup, rebuilding engines or fixing just about anything around the house. From sinks to refrigerators, people are always looking for a way to fix things themselves so that they don't have to spend thousands of dollars hiring someone to come out to their house and take care of it for them. The key to success with this type of internet income is marketing. We already talked about those social media outlets in the e-book section. You can utilize those to market your YouTube videos as well. Making the video itself is not as easy as it sounds, but it can be quite a bit of fun. There will be some trial and error, and once it's done there will be some editing involved, but it is free to post videos to YouTube meaning no upfront cost. You'll only need to put the time and energy into creating your YouTube masterpiece.

The last topic we'll go over for internet income is creating an online course or an online guide. Is there something that you are particularly great at? Perhaps you know a lot about medieval history, how to rebuild a transmission for a particular or rare car, or maybe you can teach people how to sell real estate. Really, whatever you are good at and/or passionate about, you can create a course to help others who might be looking to expand their own knowledge base.

While there are a few platforms in which you can do this, one of the best-known platforms is Udemy.com. They have over *eight million* students looking to learn something new every day. That is a huge number of people to whom you can sell your product. What's great about this is there isn't a whole lot you need to do in the way of marketing. Udemy has it all categorized. You would want to write a killer description of your tutorial, though. That way, you would have a bit of an advantage over others who might be teaching related online courses. This is literally something you can make money at while you sleep. Your course can include a video, tutorials, lessons and checklists. What's great about Udemy is you can make it your own. There are even several price points for this website meaning you can have a higher price point that has all the bells and whistles and then lower price points that have a little less, but still the same great information you are providing at the higher price. This makes it so you can market to a larger group of people maximizing your potential for passive income.

Finally, you can make an online guide. Again, the possibilities here are endless. You can create a guide to the best fishing in the country, white water rafting, skiing...whatever you'd like. Online guides don't usually cost anything to the person searching for those items. Where you make your money with guides is through advertisers. If you are creating a guide to fishing, you'd want to check with bait shops and any outdoorsy type retail place that would want to place an ad on your site. Some pay by the click, others pay if someone purchases something through their website after clicking from your guide. It depends on the retailer, but this is a great way to earn passive income. What's not to love about sharing your expertise and making money in the process?

We've covered quite a few things in this opening chapter! We have outlined just a few of the ways you can earn a passive income using the internet. One of the best things about the things we talked about is they can be fun, especially if writing or photography is a hobby. Taking surveys probably isn't how you picture yourself spending your weekend, but when it comes to passive income, you have to admit that clicking through a survey or getting paid to play a new online game is pretty passive. That being said, there are much more ways and exploring those is just a Google search away. Find something that interests you and the sky is the limit.

Chapter 2 – Passive Income Earned From Investing

Investing may sound daunting. It's highly likely you are looking to passive income as a way to make money because you don't have a lot of excess cash laying around. Let's face it…the majority of us don't. While investing may sound intimidating and expensive, rest assured there are ways to earn a passive income without having to put a second mortgage on your house or dip into your children's college funds.

One of the first things you can look at in the way of investing is joining a Lending Club. This is a web-based lending program geared toward peer to peer borrowing and lending. Unlike traditional investing in US Treasury Securities or bank certificates, Lending Clubs offer a much higher yield on returns. Bonds and other bank certificates usually earn about one-percent which is passive income in the basest of terms. Making that little every year won't do much in the way of helping you retire sooner or get to that beach house you've been looking to vacation at for the past few years. Lending Clubs have a much higher interest rate and with that comes an increased risk. Like bank loans, those given through a Lending Club are at risk of default meaning if the borrower doesn't repay the note to you, that's money you've just lost on investment.

The risk of a defaulted loan is minimal if you know what kinds of loans are more likely to be paid back. For example, you wouldn't want to invest in a mom and pop coffee shop that is slotted for location in the midst of several big chain coffee shops. While that is a risk that can pay off, it might be a little too risky for your liking. And that's okay! When it comes to investing, you have to do what makes you comfortable. Especially when we are talking about putting up some of your own, hard-earned money. Remember, the thought of doing that might make you a little uneasy, but the payoff can be very rewarding.

Lending Clubs usually recommend you start out with an initial deposit of around 2500.00. You can invest as little as twenty-five dollars on a single loan, meaning you can actually invest in up to one-hundred businesses at a time. The potential for earning passive income using this method is higher, and you are invested in businesses that you didn't have to put all your blood, sweat and tears into starting up. That's pretty passive and far less stressful. The beautiful thing about Lending Clubs is there are several that are free to join. That's great if you know a good chunk of what you do have saved is going to go to the initial deposit.

In terms of investing, you can also look into Index Funds. It is a form of mutual fund that helps you to invest in the stock market in an entirely passive manner. These is especially great because you don't have to concern yourself with choosing an investment, knowing when to buy or sell, or rebalancing your portfolio. All of those things are handled by the index fund.

One of the best sites to set up an index fund is Scottrade. Their website is easy to maneuver, setting up an account is pretty affordable. Their website offers levels of investment and depending on how much you invest; you'll also be rewarded with a minimum of fifty free trades. It's a pretty awesome deal. Not to mention, you get to choose where your money goes. Also, if you set up with Scottrade and decide to invest in a different manner, you'll already have an account established with them. Along the same lines as investing, if you are looking to get a retirement fund going (outside of a traditional 401k you may have through your full-time job), Roth IRA's are a great place to put your money. And, if you leave your job you can roll your 401k into a Roth IRA without having to pay huge tax penalties.

Another way to invest online is the use of a Robo-advisor. If you are worried about trying to decipher stocks and how the market works, let a Robo-advisor do the job for you. One Robo-advisor that gets some of the best reviews is Betterment. You provide them with the funds, and their algorithms will find the best investments for you. In addition to that, it will keep your portfolio balanced. Talk about passive! While there is the upfront cost of investing, you won't have to stress over reading the paper or watching the news every day to see where your stocks are at.

One of the most well-known and popular ways of investing is in the Real Estate Market. As with most investments, this can come with some risk, and there are more ways to invest in Real Estate than just flipping houses or turning them into rental properties. Because rental properties are the most common, we will discuss them in a little greater detail.

Real Estate rentals aren't entirely passive income makers. There is some work involved in finding the house or apartment complex, but once you've found a property and rented it out, you'll only need to make sure your tenant sends you a rent check every month. You can also hire property management companies to manage your rental for you. Their typical fee is approximately ten-percent of the rental amount every month. One of the benefits of rental properties is once the original loan is paid off, your earnings go up substantially. If you have more than one property that's paid off and bringing in decent rent each month, you might even be able to retire and turn your investments into full-fledged passive income.

Along the same lines, you can also invest in Real Estate Investment

Trusts, also known as REITs. As previously mentioned, investing in real estate itself isn't entirely passive. However, if you want to invest in real estate completely passively, REITs are the way to go. This is kind of like investing in a mutual fund with various real estate projects as opposed to stocks or bonds. Like mutual funds, REITs are managed by professionals, so you won't have to worry about learning all the legalities of real estate. REITs pay a higher dividend than most bonds, stocks or even bank investments. You can also sell your REIT at any time making it a more fluid form of passive income since you'll never actually have to invest in an actual property.

There is one final note we'll mention in regards to real estate. If you already own your own home and have some space available, you can rent out that unused space on Airbnb. It's a relatively new concept, but over the past year, it has exploded all around the globe. This engine allows people to travel all over the world and stay places much cheaper than hotels, hostels or traditional bed and breakfasts. By signing up for Airbnb, you can earn money simply by renting out your unused space to travelers. Obviously, there is some risk involved, but Airbnb has a community safety and standards expectations for people renting their space as well as those seeking places to stay. A form of government-issued identification is required so there isn't much to worry about in the way of hosting a felon.

The site provides income examples, and a relatively easy search showed that one room in Denver, Colorado can go for as much as 250.00 per week. Not bad for passive income and the best part about this is, you already *own* the investment property.

Chapter 3 – Start a Blog

There are many things you can do with a blog, but we'll focus on two. Creating your own and buying an existing blog. Creating your own won't be entirely passive, but once again, it is easier than finding a part-time job. And with most passive income internet based ventures, you can do this from the comfort of your couch. You aren't going to miss out on cherished family time or dinner because you had to go from your full-time job to the part-time job.

The trick to blogging is consistency. Thousands of blogs are created every year, and the majority of them are abandoned within a few months. Blogging is a competitive market and if it is something you choose to do, remember to stay consistent, post on a regular basis, market using other social media sites we've discussed previously. Passive income from blogging comes mostly from advertisements. Those big-time advertisers are looking for blogs that get a lot of traffic to advertise their product. This will require some work at the beginning with posting, marketing and reaching out to advertisers to get them to pay you to advertise on your blog. If you like to write, or you have an idea for something that's funny tech savvy, or just completely different, blogging is a great way to earn that semi-passive income.

To be clear, one can't expect to make decent passive income by writing and publishing any old blog. In my quest to find what people are most interested in reading about, I came across a list of a whopping *eighty-one* ideas for writing a blog that will sell. We won't be covering all, but I'm going to list the top ten.

1. **Self-improvement and Self-hypnosis**. Whether you go into a bookstore or are looking for books online, self-improvement is one that piques a lot of people's interest. No one is perfect, and most people are looking for a way to improve themselves. Whether it'd be through physical fitness or having a more positive attitude in life, there are literally hundreds, if not thousands of self-improvement topics to blog about. Self-hypnosis is incredibly interesting. It isn't what you think, either. We've all seen the silly reality shows where people using hypnosis make their subjects act out of sorts. Self-hypnosis in this context actually goes hand in hand with self-improvement. Self-hypnosis is about meditating your way to a different you. Whether you need to boost your self-

esteem or work on confidence and overall outlook on life, self-hypnosis is something that people are highly interested in.

2. **Health and Fitness for Busy People**. This is kind of along the same lines as self-improvement. Many people want to get in better shape, but who really has the time? A blog about fitness for people who are always on the go (and not working on earning passive incomes like we are) would be a great target audience. Plus, many sports and activity retailers would love to pay to advertise on a site that is suggesting people get into shape. Everything they need to attain their goals is a click away…from *your* blog.

3. **Language and Learning Blogs**. These can be lumped in with creating that online course we discussed earlier. As a matter of fact, should you choose to teach a course, you could include blogs from your personal site as part of the learner's course and content. The language might be a little more difficult if you are only fluent in one, but learning new things always appeals to people.

4. **Earning extra money**. Who better to write a blog about this subject than you? You're well on your way to earning passive income without having to get a second job, right? There are quite a few blogs that discuss passive income, but there aren't many that

detail trials, tribulations, and successes. It'd be a nice little niche for you to slide right into.

5. **Food blogs**. We aren't talking about the local pub or fast food chain. Specialty or unique/rare foods are what interests people. "Foodie" blogs come and go, but the same applies here as it did with fitness. Rating food and restaurants in a way that gets people to read your blog over others will entice advertisers to pay for space on your blog. And, you get to go out and try all kinds of amazing new foods. Sounds like a win-win situation.

So, we've talked about creating your own blog, but what if you aren't interested in writing them yourself? Perhaps you don't quite have the time to invest in doing some research and writing the blog, then finding advertisers for your site. That's okay; there is another way to earn a passive income by purchasing a pre-existing blog. The interesting thing about this idea is all the content is there. You will have to put some effort into maintaining the site, but all the bare bones are set up for you.

A lot of blogs use Google AdSense, which is what provides a monthly income for a blogger. It is based on the ads Google places on their site or blog. Blogs tend to sell for approximately twenty-four times their average monthly income. For instance, if a blog earns two-hundred and fifty dollars per month, the most you'll pay for that blog is three-thousand dollars. Like we mentioned in the chapter about investing in real estate, some things will require a bit of money up front. If you are able to afford this route with buying a blog, keep in mind that if the site is generating two-fifty per month, you will earn your money back in a year. After that, the blog will be making money that will be all profit. With a little effort put into the blog to make sure content remains up to date, it'll be mostly passive and something you can do in your spare time.

Chapter 4 – Selling Products Online

There are a couple of ways to make money by selling products online to earn a passive income. Actually, there are several, but the point of this book is passive income, so we will stick to discussing two great ways to make that money using a website. Drop ship products for another retailer, or sell your own products online. If you don't want to invest a lot of money in products to stock your online store, drop shipping might be more appealing. In this chapter, we will cover both so you can get a good idea as to what will work best for you and fit into your budget.

Drop shipping isn't entirely passive, but it's one of the closest things you can to do earn that passive income. What is it, you ask? Drop shipping is where a product goes directly from the manufacturer to the customer. And, where do you fit into this equation? You would be the middle man. Drop shipping requires a little effort in that you'd need to set up a website to sell a product. What's particularly significant about this is, you don't have to spend the time creating a product, then marketing it online, calculating sales, paying people to help you out…none of that. The middle man in this scenario simply has the product on their site, and when people arrive to purchase, the order is either automatically or manually forwarded to the manufacturer. The product is then "drop shipped" to the customer. This means you will never have to get your hands dirty. The passive income part of this scenario comes from your earning a percentage of the sales of whatever product or products you have on your website.

In addition to simply being the middle man, let's talk about some other benefits to using drop shipping as your passive income source. One of the biggest advantages is that the startup for this is minuscule, especially compared to some of the other things we've mentioned such as real estate and purchasing a blog. You will also be able to offer an extensive selection and wide variety of products without ever having to purchase the product, store it, then pay to have it shipped to the customer.

The risk is reduced tremendously with drop shipping. Most retailers who set up a website and sell the product have to invest hundreds or even thousands of dollars up front to build their inventory. Drop shipping requires you purchase the product only briefly, then have it shipped directly to the customer. The upfront cost of drop shipping is pretty minimal. You also don't need to worry about renting space to house the product. The store you own is virtual which means you can run your drop ship business from the comfort of your own home. Or, anywhere that has wifi.

What's important to mention about drop shipping is if you want to be successful, you'll need to find a specialized niche. In order to do well with drop shipping, you'll want to do a little research and find retailers that utilize that service. Don't narrow yourself to one or two markets. In the beginning, start small, but the more you are able to expand and the more products you are able to add to your website, the more likely you are to earn a pretty decent passive income.

When it comes to selling your own products on the internet, the possibilities are endless. Online, you can sell any service or product that you can think of. It could be anything from a product you've created, things of a digital nature like software or DVDs, even instructional videos if you have them. If not, this is a great opportunity for you to create them, as discussed in the section regarding Udemy or YouTube videos.

If you don't have want to setup your own website, you can work with affiliates who are willing to sell your product for you. In this instance, it would be like your partner is the drop shipper or middle man and you are the retailer. Either way is perfectly acceptable and a great way to earn a passive income.

How much money you make depends on how much time you are willing to commit to this venture. One story that is particularly intriguing is that of a woman who was able to quit her job and earn one-hundred thousand dollars a year with her online store. Now, let's be clear that this isn't the norm. The reason she was able to make so much money was that she'd found that special niche. Her online store specializes in making handkerchiefs for special occasions like weddings. They don't just produce handkerchiefs, though. They make linen party favor bags, lace umbrellas, pillowcases and much more. That is the kind of idea that will earn significant money. Get those wheels in your head spinning! Undoubtedly you've had some magnificent ideas for products that are unique or even those that would simplify your daily life.

Along these lines, you can also set up a website to sell products that you are familiar with. This is similar to selling your own product except you don't have to create a product...you'll be selling someone else's product. With this concept, you could start out small with one or two products, and after a while, you can add other products that are closely related to what you've already begun to sell. You'd want to make the products similar to avoid needing a large website to sell hundreds of products. Keeping your site neat, clean and straightforward will bring more traffic.

Chapter 5 – Affiliate Marketing

When it comes to passive income, the majority of people who get into it start out in affiliate marketing. While the concept has been around for quite some time, it became popular after the 4-Hour Work Week was released. Ever since then, people have been excited to find a way to "make money while they sleep." The idea behind affiliate marketing is you earn a commission by promoting other people's products. You make money when a sale is completed thanks to your marketing. This relies heavily on revenue sharing, which can go either way. That means that if you have a product and are looking to sell more of it, you can offer promoters financial incentive for marketing your product. Alternatively, if you do not have a product of your own, you can still make money by promoting a product you believe in or are familiar with.

In this chapter, we are going to get into detail as to what affiliate marketing is and how you can get started earning passive income by using it.

Conversely, there are three or four sides to affiliate marketing, depending on which definition you are looking at. For all intents and purposes, when it comes down to it, there are really only two sides to this marketing equation. There are the product seller and creator on the one hand and the marketer on the other. In affiliate marketing, you can be both the creator and the marketer and profit from 'shared' revenue.

Let's take a closer look at all the working parts of what makes affiliate marketing such a successful venture.

There is the merchant, who can also be the creator, seller, retailer, brand or vendor. Ultimately, the merchant is the creator of the product. For example, Dyson vacuum cleaners. On a smaller scale, it can be a person who creates and sells online courses to people wishing to further their education without having to go back to college. From the solo entrepreneur to online startup companies and even Fortune 500 companies, just about anyone can be the merchant who is behind the affiliate marketing system. The merchant doesn't have to be actively involved. They only have to be able to offer a product to sell.

The next party is the affiliate who is also sometimes referred to as the publisher. Like the merchant, the affiliate can be an entire company or an individual. The affiliate is where the marketing happens. They are the party responsible for promoting one or several products in an attempt to attract and even convince those potential customers that the product is needed or of great value and the customer winds up purchasing this product because of the marketing. One way this type of marketing is achieved is by a review of the product being sold with a blog. Really, this can be done on any social media outlet and Facebook is getting to be a huge platform for affiliate marketing. Perhaps you hadn't noticed it before, but you likely will now. Maybe one of your friends posted something about a product they liked. If you went to that website and bought a product, your friend might have been compensated and would be the affiliate.

Now, while there are two parties to the actual functionality of affiliate marketing, there is one key component to recognize, and that is the customer. Without people to consume the product, there would be no need for affiliate marketing, right?

The consumer or customer might be unaware that they are involved in affiliate marketing. That depends on how the affiliate markets the product. Some affiliates let their customers know up front that they are trying to sell a particular product. Others are more passive in using ads or links in their blogs for people to follow to certain websites. No matter how the consumer gets to the product, the affiliate is paid a commission if there is a sale, so long as there is an agreement between the affiliate and the merchant. Nine times out of ten, there is some sort of arrangement between the two parties. Most people don't tend to push a product without having an incentive to do so. Whether the affiliate gets paid in free product or cold hard cash is something to be worked out between the marketer and affiliate. If you choose to be an affiliate for a product to earn passive income, make sure your contract is clear so that no matter which form of payment is received, you will actually be compensated for your time and effort in marketing the product.

At the beginning of this chapter, we talked about three to four components to affiliate marketing. Because most people only see three true components, we will not go into too much detail with the fourth. However, it should be mentioned, albeit briefly.

The fourth component is the network. In most cases, the network acts as an intermediary between the merchant and the affiliate. The network tends to handle payment between the merchant and the affiliate. They can also be responsible for shipping and delivery of the product being sold. The use of a network is not required, although some bigger corporations tend to use the networks to promote, ship and deliver their product. A good example of a network is Amazon. That website sells everything you can think of from tools and books to toys and household items. They have an Amazon Associate program that allows you to promote any item you sell on their platform. Of course, Amazon charges a fee for this, though it is usually pretty minimal.

Now, there are four simple steps to becoming either a merchant or an affiliate. Most people begin with affiliate because it is slightly easier than starting out as a merchant. We will provide you with the four steps for each so that you can make an informed decision as to which route you'd prefer to take to start earning your passive income.

Becoming an Online Merchant in 4 steps:

1. You need to have an idea for a product. This is tough because many people have it in their head that coming up with an idea is hard, which isn't necessarily true. What happens with most people is they have an idea that they are in love with and that is where the problem is. They become too focused on that *one* idea. To get started as a merchant, you'll want to find products out there that are already selling well, but that the market isn't already flooded with. You need something that people will want to buy and will be able to use on a daily basis. Perhaps you have an idea that will make household chores easier or a product that can clean as well as bleach without all the toxic fumes. Take a little bit of time and do some research on Google to find ideas or products you can get behind.

2. The second step is to validate your idea. You wouldn't want to make or back a product without knowing that there would be

reasonable interest for people to purchase it. Ask family, friends, work associates…anyone you know will be *honest* with you about the product you are looking to sell. Sometimes, that can be tough with family and friends because they want to support you in your ventures. Make sure you are asking people you know will tell you the absolute truth.

3. Create your product or prepare to market the already established product you've decided to sell. Creating products can be costly up front. However, if you've done research, had plenty of people tell you they'd definitely buy it and you are passionate about it, go for it!

4. Finally, once your product is ready, you'll need to find the affiliates willing to sell and market your product on your behalf.

Becoming an Online Affiliate in 4 steps:

1. First and foremost, start reviewing the products in your chosen niche. You can do this via YouTube, a blog or live streams on a platform like Periscope.

2. Collect emails so that you can connect with your audience.

3. Check out joint venture webinars. It is a great platform to make a lot of sales in a shorter period of time. At the same time, you'll be growing your email list and expanding your customer base.

4. Finally, once you get your affiliate business to a point where it is making money you can scale growth by using pay per click advertising.

To recap, there are two ways to get into affiliate marketing; becoming an affiliate or becoming a merchant. With what we've outlined here today, I'm positive you'll be able to find which route works best for you. Perhaps you'll discover you can do both!

Chapter 6 – Venture Capitalism

Investopedia defines venture capitalism as a person who provides capital for startup ventures or one who supports small companies that want to expand but lack access to equities markets. Venture capitalists are people who are willing to invest in these companies because they know they will earn significant returns on the companies if they are successful. There is some risk in investing in companies that are in the startup phase because most new businesses fail within the first year. If it is a risk you are financially able to take, it's an easy way to earn a passive income. The venture capitalist provides the money up front, and when the business succeeds, they get to sit back and relax while the money rolls in.

While there are several paths to becoming a venture capitalist, there are two that are most common and, quite frankly, the simplest to get into. Serial entrepreneurship and tech-oriented investment banking.

The serial entrepreneur differs from a typical entrepreneur in that they will come up with an idea for business, get it started, and then hand the reigns over to someone else. An entrepreneur that is not serial will start a business, get it through the first year and beyond and stick with it until they retire or sell the business. Typically, they do not start more than one business whereas a serial entrepreneur will do this several times throughout their business life. This is ideal for people who have lots of great ideas and want to share them with the world. Once the business is up and running, the serial entrepreneur will earn a passive income from all the businesses they get started. Like many forms of passive income and as we've mentioned a time or two, getting on the road to passive income will take some work. Ultimately, when you are earning money without having to leave your home, whatever you put into the idea, in the beginning, will clearly be worth it.

In addition to the ability to spot a great investment from a mile away, a serial entrepreneur is also great at motivating people and inspiring others to follow them. They are willing to take a personal and business risk. They have the ability to recognize a great market to invest in consistently. Some people have made their career being a serial entrepreneur. Realistically, you could help several businesses get their start, which would not be passive. However, once those businesses are up, running and making good money, all you have to do is sit back and enjoy the fruits of your labor. And that, my friend, is the definition of passive income.

The second is the tech-oriented investment banker. Of the two, this is becoming less common because the risk associated is higher. An investment banker, in general, is someone who provides the capital for business...any business. Now, as we have mentioned previously, for this section, we are specifically talking about tech-oriented investments. These tend to be a little less risky because of the way technology is evolving. People are always looking for the next new, really impressive technological advancement. For this type of venture capitalism, you would invest in some kind of emerging technology, and when it succeeds, you will get to reap the rewards of getting in on this investment on the ground floor. As we have talked about previously, finding a specific niche or even an area of technology in which you are particularly well versed is a great way to keep your risk a little lower. That being said, you probably would not want to invest in several tech companies right away. The point of passive income is earned money with less stress than having to go out and find a part-time job. Do a little research on emerging technologies and find the one you are most confident in.

As we've gone over a few times so far, any kind of investing comes with risk. Of the two most common forms of investing through venture capitalism, you are more likely to succeed and experience less risk with serial entrepreneurship. That being said, if you are very tech savvy and can recognize a great product easily, go that route. Remember, you are trying to get yourself to a point where you are earning that passive income, and that means finding exactly what is going to work best for you.

PART 2

PASSIVE INCOME—A FUTURE OF FINANCIAL FREEDOM

You've just come home from a beautiful week spent on the beach, or an active adventure vacation spent hiking, exploring and letting your imaginations run free, and now it's time to return to the real world. If you're letting passive income work for you while you were away, you're not dreading coming home to a stack of bills and a diminished bank account. Instead, you can't wait to come back and check your accounts to see how much money you made during your time away. Sound like a fantasy? It doesn't have to be. That's what passive income is all about—it should work harder than you do.

Don't let anyone blow smoke up your behind when it comes to enjoying all the financial freedom that having several streams of passive income can create for you. Let me clarify a few very important points about the realities of passive income. First of all, creating avenues of passive income isn't a "get rich quick" trendy scheme that requires no work on your part. In fact, developing diverse pathways of passive income can be quite challenging and isn't very passive in the beginning.

Sorry for being a buzzkill, but to understand the actual advantages that building significant passive income can provide, it's necessary that you, perhaps, change your perspective. Look at our title to this book. You may have missed one vital word—future. To build passive income takes an investment of time and money upfront. To create financial freedom down the road, you need to be willing to do what others refuse to do—work harder, save, and invest your extra money in building a future that makes that fantasy scenario we started with a reality.

To better understand what passive income is, let's examine what it is not. Passive income is not a second or part-time job. After all, that would just be creating more of what you already have, right? If you are working a 9-5 job, trading time for money, you are limited to the amount of money you can make. There is only so many hours in a day—only so much time you can devote to making more money, whether that is overtime or another part-time job to supplement your regular income. This is known as "active" income.

Passive income follows a whole different set of rules than active income. Once you have discovered the passive income avenues you wish to pursue, and once you have made your initial investment of time and money, then real passive income continues to work for you while you move on to something else. You can and should have many avenues of passive income, track them frequently, and determine which ones generate the highest and most consistent returns. It's different for everyone. One of the most incredible differences between active and passive income is the surprising amount of money you can generate. What you have to look forward to is that eventually, you'll be putting very little effort into maintaining the source of that income. The truth is, passive income is only limited by your imagination.

For those of you who feel more secure with a definition—passive income is the money earned that continues to roll in with very little to no effort required after your initial upfront investment of time and money. A stream of passive income is when your focus moves from one source to many sources, to diversify your efforts and increase your successful returns, even if one or two streams are not currently producing the results you expected.

What Can Passive Income Do for You?

We've already determined your passive income is going to work for your "future" financial freedom, so it's necessary not to expect instant gratification, right? Wrong! Once you begin seeing the results of your passive income streams working on your behalf, you'll feel gratified seeing your money multiply. What you'll learn are ways to manage and control your future that you never thought yourself capable of doing. One success will build upon another until your confidence and increased feelings of self-worth will be almost as rewarding as the additional income you are generating. Here are some of the things you can expect when you have created several successful streams of passive income.

- You have the freedom to work on what you feel passionate about rather than being trapped by a 9-5 job with limited monetary gain and even less personal gratification.

- You can plan to retire early, explore magnificent world class destinations that you may never have had the opportunity to do without your passive income.

- You can spend more time with your family and not continue to be a slave to your job.

- You can help others and volunteer for heartfelt causes.

- You can live a healthier, stress-free life.

- You can let your imagination and creative spirit run wild—writing the next best seller, painting on the beach, or exploring faraway lands and people.

- Bottom line—you can live the life of those you currently envy!

Sounds Good—But Where Do You Start?

I would love to say that you have already started by reading this book, but I'd be remiss if I didn't explain a sad fact. Many people read about creating passive income, and that is all the further they get to achieving it. Either they think they don't have the skills or knowledge, or they lack the motivation to do what it takes today to plan for a better tomorrow. Don't be one of those people. Every new endeavor comes with an initial energy and inner spark that excites and inspires you. Unfortunately, if that initial spark isn't attended to, it will not grow into a raging fire that spurs you to continue to work all the avenues of passive income that could create financial freedom. The enthusiasm you may be feeling as you read these pages needs to be protected and nurtured—worked into a viable fuel that speeds your progress. It's not only important to know how to start, but you must know how to push yourself through some of the more demanding up-front challenges of creating passive income. You must be "active" in your pursuit of "passive" income.

Here are three tips to help you get a good start in building a stream of passive income.

1. Ask yourself why you want to do this? Are you only in it for the money, or would you like to do something for which you feel passion? Very important question. Many of the streams of passive income you will be interested in pursuing will require passionately presenting your ideas to others. People can spot a "huckster' a mile away, so whatever you choose to do, make it something you believe in and enjoy. Don't just

make it an idea or product you need to push off on people to make money.

2. If you don't have much money to invest in the beginning, that's okay. However, count on spending a good deal of time in planning and preparing to take your product or service to market and make it a success. Take the time to consider your consumer, to understand their needs and wants so that you make sure your choice will be beneficial and long-lasting. If you are working a full-time job while you're getting your passive income going, know that you may not have a lot of time to be a Sunday afternoon couch potato anymore.

3. Realize that there is no such thing as passive income that is 100% passive, no matter how much planning and preparation you have given it. Even investments in stocks require you to check on the market and frequently buy and sell to optimize your investment. If you've chosen eBooks, blogs, websites, or apps, you still need to continue to produce so you have a pipeline of possibilities. Though maintenance may be minimal as your passive income matures, you'll still want to devote time to new endeavors. If you are passionate about

what you are doing, you'll enjoy the process as much as the end results (1).

Some passive income streams require a substantial amount of money to start. If those are the types of passive income that flip your switch, you'll need to save some money first. For example, if real estate or stocks are what interests you, then you have two way to begin. Either you win the lottery or inherit, or you do it the old-fashioned way and save. Instead of having a Christmas or vacation fund, you may want to start a passive income fund. Save a little out of your check each month and sock it away. Consider cleaning out your garage and having a large yard sale. Take the proceeds from the sale, and begin investing just a little to get your feet wet. Once you experience some success, you can take your profit and reinvest, building and diversifying your investments.

That word "diversify" is crucial when it comes to planning what type of passive incomes to choose. There is wisdom in the adage, "Don't put all your eggs in one basket." If you have several different things working for you, when demand is down for one, it may be up for another. Plus, who wants to do the same thing over and over, when you could be enjoying exploring different things every day? Leave that for your 9-5 job. Speaking of which, the earlier you can begin building an ongoing stream of passive income, the better. Waiting until you retire to decide whether you'll have enough money to retire comfortably, is like leaving your car windows rolled down in a rain storm and worrying if your seats will get wet. Of course, they will!

Sure, if you're retired, you'll have all the time in the world to invest in building passive income—but, no money. Even the smallest of ventures usually requires some monetary investment. Waiting until you're older to think about your future is never a good idea.

So, where and when do you start? There's no time like right now. Here are five easy steps to get started on building a steady stream of passive income.

Step #1:

Make a list of things you love to do. Include hobbies, unique talents you possess, creative outlets you have, or perhaps objects you have collected over the years.

Step #2:

Write down what you feel would be a comfortable and believable amount of money for you to make in a year's time with your stream of passive income.

Step #3:

Now compare the two steps, looking at what you could do that would contribute to your goal. For example: If your goal was to make $10,000 per year in passive income, what's on that list in step #1 to help you do that? Is there anything that would appeal to a significant number of people if you were to market that product or service? Let's say your hobby was to play the piano. Could you write an eBook on how to play the piano? Could you have an online course, teaching beginners how to play? Could you have YouTube lessons that would complement your book, demonstrating a step-by-step course? Could you have a website offering several beginner books or beginner sheet music for sale that would best help the beginner? Could you hold a webinar to teach several enrollees to play at once, charging a reasonable fee, of course?

Once you've given full reign to your imagination, the list of possible products and services are endless. The key is to let your mind run with wild abandon to all the possibilities. Make sure you write them all down, no matter how silly they might sound. Somewhere inside the silliness might just be an amazing way to earn passive income.

Step #4:

Start small. If you need inventory for your passive income, don't buy a warehouse full and then pay to have it stored—test the waters. In case this particular type of passive income was not successful, you don't want to lose too much on a fail. There will be some things in which you invest time and money, which go anywhere. Don't get discouraged. All it could mean is that you need to do a better job of planning and preparing before investing the time and money.

Step #5:

Involve a well-wisher. What I mean by this is, solicit the support of someone who cares about your success. If it's a close family member, make sure they will benefit from the sacrifices they will be asked to make as well. For instance, if you are investing your previously free time or some of your family time to work on your own ventures, then an involved spouse will be less likely to burden you with complaints. Share your goals and get that person aboard right from the get go so their participation can help minimize your time investment.

Most importantly, believe in pursuing passive. If you have things on your list that you like but don't believe anybody else would, it's probably not going to be an excellent addition to your stream of passive income. It might be better to postpone that one until you have some successes under your belt. Early success is excellent inspiration for continued activity. Even though your ideas may be out of the norm, that's the great thing about passive income. Nothing's off limits. If your idea sounds too far out there, find an expert that you respect in the field of your interest, and let that expert help you get grounded. Who knows, with just a little help your idea could go from far out to far-reaching, attracting others to your cause or venture.

With expectations intact, now give all these things some thought and continue reading to see some specifics on how to make your passive income prosperous.

CHAPTER 1: 10 POPULAR SOURCES OF PASSIVE INCOME

Almost anything can become a source of passive income, so what you choose to include in your stream should be what excites you— what you feel passionate about so that you can enjoy the journey of building a financially free future. Learn to think about passive income differently. It's not a job, not an obligation or responsibility; it's more like a fun hobby that happens to earn you money. The more you enjoy working on building a passive income, the more you'll succeed at creating something special that will attract consumers.

Although we are going to suggest ten sources that others have found to be profitable and exciting, your sources of passive income are only limited by the bounds of your creativity. This chapter will introduce you to some tried and proven streams of passive income. In the chapters to follow, we will go into depth on how to begin building each one of these sources. The exciting thing about passive income is that you get to take a source, explore and expand all the possibilities of turning that source into a stream of revenue, and discover how you can motivate and inspire others to join in, participating in the adventure because they believe in you and your offering.

The following ten sources of passive income have helped many beginners build their financial futures, but it does come at a cost. Typically, the more money you invest, the less time it requires to maintain the stream. However, many of the suggested sources don't require a great deal of monetary investment, so don't think you must have a sizeable nest egg before starting your stream of passive income. Be prepared, though, to spend your spare time away from the television and into ways you can generate avenues of income.

10 Sources of Passive Income

1. Writing eBooks

   You don't have to be an excellent writer to build a pipeline of eBooks that will earn you money while you move forward with other sources. All you need to do is find topics you know enough about to help or interest others. Great subject matter is key to success in eBooks. Once you have established topics you think readers would enjoy and benefit from, you're halfway there. We'll show you how to start a pipeline of eBooks without ever writing a word.

2. Developing Apps

Again, you don't have to be an expert programmer to design and develop an incredible app that would be useful to others. As we go, we'll show you how you can hire the work done efficiently and competently, and get onto making money. We'll teach you how to identify a problem and create a solution with your app. You'll learn how to design and market your app so that users will be eager to see what's coming next. It won't just stop with one app. Once you learn the process, you'll begin to think like a real problem solver. Soon, you'll be an expert at discovering and designing apps that help people in their day-to-day lives. Creating passive income through the development of apps can be a rewarding endeavor—both financially and emotionally!

3. Creating Blogs

    When you are building your sources of passive income, you'll want to do so with things in which you are already familiar. Don't worry if you are not yet an expert, once you've completed your research and discovery, you can tap into all the experts' information and learn to organize it in a way that is unique, interesting, and easy for consumers to follow. Highly intelligent people are not experts at everything, they simply know how to surround themselves with other very smart individuals who are experts, and then they tap into that expert knowledge and skill to build their own success.

    Blogs are a way to create a following where readers recognize the value of the information you impart. Think of blogs as a vehicle in which to deliver information and inspire people to continue to learn more about the topic you have chosen.

You're the teacher, gathering eager students whose goal is to absorb all your knowledge and skills and apply your expertise.

4. Developing Websites

    Again, don't worry about not knowing how to write code or develop a website. You just need to be the idea person. Yours is to create and inspire; let others who are expert web developers activate your ideas. We'll show you in a later chapter all the amazing things you can do with a website that works while you're not.

5. Investing in Stocks

    Some people think they must have a lot of money and knowledge to invest in stocks. That's a myth. Remember what I said about starting small and then letting your investments work for you. When you invest a little, chances are you're not going to make an overnight killing on a magical rise in your stock's value. You'll invest a little, and you'll make a little, and then you'll reinvest a little more until you build up that nest egg. Keep your energy invested in the journey, and for the moment, don't worry about the end destination.

6. Investing in Bonds

    Investing in bonds is a long-term endeavor. Although this is almost the purest form of passive income, it is also one in which your mindset must be about "future" financial freedom. Bonds are slow growing but typically very steady and reliable.

7. Buying Annuities

    Buying annuities can be tricky. As we introduce this source of income, we'll give you tips on what to buy and what to avoid. We'll discuss the pros and cons of buying annuities so that you can decide whether this source of passive income is right for you.

8. Creating Rental Income

    Many people believe this source of passive income requires $25,000 or more to purchase a rental property, but we'll teach you how to build rental income with minimal investments of time and money. This is a source that is wide open for innovative thinkers. Rental opportunities are typically growing investments with excellent returns. Notice I didn't say stable? There's no such thing as stable when it comes to passive income. If your source is stable, you're losing money.

9. Buying Mortgages

Think of these as paper exchanges. You can buy others' mortgages or even become a private lender. This source of passive income can be quite profitable and require little time, but you will need to have some financial backing to begin. This may be one that you'll want to start after you've had some success with your other sources.

10. Product Development and Resale

Anybody can do this, and it can be a lot of fun. We'll show you how the experts have learned to buy low and sell high. You'll learn to recognize the right products, maintain the proper working inventory, and track your success. Keep your eyes and ears open, and you might also invent a whole new product or service that excites consumers enough to follow you and see what spinoffs may occur.

Using several of these sources, and perhaps more that you find particularly interesting will prepare you for incredible success in building a productive stream of passive income. The reason we suggest many sources, and a variety of ways to use those sources, is because the more sources used, the greater chance you have for success. If one source in the stream fails to produce, go to another. If one source does well for you and then slows to a crawl, it will give you time to focus on other things. Rarely does passive income stream steady, so you ride one while you continue to develop another and another.

That's what makes passive income so different from a regular 9-5 job; you're not stuck in one field or industry. Instead, you can explore and expand your thinking; creativity is the name of the game. Your innovations can be richly rewarding. Instead of being frustrated by short-sighted, status quo superiors who cannot appreciate maverick thinkers like you, you'll find great satisfaction in coming up with new sources of passive income and exciting ways to make those sources work for you.

Remember, you are erecting a platform from which to launch your passive income portfolio. The more sources used, the greater the stream of passive income you will create. Hanging in there for long-term profits is key. Beginning small and building is smart. Creating sources of income with a visionary plan will prepare you for the challenges, setbacks, and successes you will experience along the way. The journey can be bumpy and sometimes the mountain of issues you must overcome can seem insurmountable. If creating passive income happened by the snap of your fingers, there would be so many others out there doing it that the competition would kill your efforts.

This is the perfect time to discuss the advantages of embracing that competitive spirit. We're not talking about the kind of competition that creates bitter rivalries that destroy or cripple one's ability to succeed. That kind of competitive spirit serves no one. However, there is a competition that teaches and inspires you to become better, to learn from others mistakes, and to help you decide how you plan to separate yourself from the pack and provide a unique product or service. So, let's examine the benefits of embracing your competition.

Five Main Benefits of Embracing Your Competition

1. Competition can create in you desire to become the best.

> Musicians having to compete for fans have created some of their most artistic work in their attempts to be better than the rest. Inventors become more innovative problem solvers when they have fierce competition. Technological engineers become more insightful to the needs of the public when their competition comes knocking at their doors. People who desire to become the best often push themselves to peak

performance.

2. Make additional discoveries in the competitive journey.

>   Because you are studying your competition to become the best, you will learn a great deal of how and why they do things the way they do. You'll also discover what NOT to do, and change the things you don't like into strategies that will help you become successful. Knowing what others are doing will enable you to engage with the consumers in a different way—in a way that makes your offering unique and allows you to stand out from the crowd.

3. Embracing your competition can save you money and time.

>   It's so much easier to learn from someone else's mistakes. There have been many times that I have saved myself money and time by learning what my competition was doing well, adopting those strategies, and then improving on them to do an even better job. Embracing and studying my competition

taught me how to work smarter and leaner. Since time means money, any time that can be saved in your startup is of significant value.

4. Competition encourages you to be more creative.

    You can get a lot of ideas from your competition and modify them to suit the way you prefer to do business. Or, you can just study what doesn't work, why consumers need something new and different, and then create that opportunity for them to shop in a broader marketplace.

5. Most of all, competition creates a need for innovative and ongoing change. Someone else will come in and do something that is different and better, then you adopt that strategy and move forward to improve on it and develop something else different and better. It's ongoing—good for consumers and good for business.

To become successful in creating a good stream of passive income you've got to do two things: a) show consumers why they need what you are offering; and, b) explain why you should be the one to provide that particular product or service. Sounds easy—but it requires thought, planning, time, and money.

CHAPTER 2: A PIPELINE OF E-BOOKS, APPS, AND BLOGS

Creating passive income from these three sources can be labor

intensive, or they can be a wonderful outlet for your creative genius.

Once you have put the upfront work in, the profits are almost

100%. With very little maintenance and no labor-intensive inventory

to worry about, you can begin making money in a matter of weeks.

Building a pipeline of e-Books, apps, and blogs can help you to

bring in immediate passive income, and you can then take some of

that profit to invest in other things.

Why Are e-Books a Good Source of Passive Income

Before you turn off to this subject because you think you don't have

the talent to write a book, think again. Remember, you don't have to

do the actual writing; you can hire that done by a professional writer.

These writers can be found in a variety of places online for a very affordable price. Sites like www.eWriterSolutions.com,

www.upworks.com, or www.outsource.com are just a few sources

where you can find excellent writers. Why belabor the writing, when

for under $250 you can have your book done in a matter of weeks?

Creating a pipeline of eBooks can give you so much flexibility in your

work. You can live anywhere that has a high-speed internet

connection for your computer and beach-front Margarita's for your

celebration when the book has been completed. Because e-Books are

digital, you don't have to worry about the cost of print, leasing a

warehouse to store inventory, or hiring employees to fulfill orders.

We'll discuss later how easy it is to get your book into the hands of

consumers.

Even though the information you have provided in your book may

be available in other locations, you've taken the time and trouble to

gather it all in one book, while putting your own unique twist on the

topic. Once you begin writing e-Books, you will soon become the

recognized expert. Link your e-Books to a regular blog posting and a

website, and you have instant marketing avenues.

The other great thing about writing e-Books is that they have a constant demand, especially if you've learned how to maintain their popularity through effective marketing strategies. This example of the amount of passive income that could be generated with e-Books will excite you. Let's say you had ten e-Books in your passive income pipeline. Now let's estimate a conservative shelf-life of twelve months for each book, and we'll set the price at $5 per book. Let's say you had interesting topics and were selling on average of 10 copies per book per day. Your six-month passive income for all ten books would be $18,250 per year.

Okay, now let's pretend you came up with great topics but did not feel comfortable in writing them yourself, so to hire a professional your writing fees would be $200 per book. Ten books at $200 would cost you a total of $2,000. There are also places online to find a designer to create a great cover for your book. Again, it may cost you $200 per book to have it done, so that would be another $2,000 for all ten books. Taking your writing and design expenses from the

$18,250 would leave you $14,250. If you choose to market your books on Amazon, it will usually cost you approximately 30% of the price of the book, which in this case would be $5,475, leaving you $8,775.

Keep in mind, the more e-Books you write, the better you market them, and the longer shelf life they have will just increase the passive income you can expect to make. Starting with only one book is fine, and you can let the proceeds you make from that one help you to pay for the next. Starting small is the way to go. However, you cannot stop after you have written just one, you'll need to keep feeding your pipeline, so the income continues.

To discover how to format your e-Books, visit https://kdp.amazon.com/help?topicId=A17W8UM0MMSQX6#format) or go online to Kindle Direct Publishing (KDP) to access the guidelines you'll need to follow to publish on Amazon or Kindle platforms. You can also use a service like Lulu that will take your uploaded e-Book and place it on multiple platforms for you, instead of you going to each site to upload. Of course, there is an additional charge for that, which is usually another percent or two of the price of your book. To use this service, simply go to https://www.lulu.com, set up your account, and upload your book (2).

If you fancy yourself a writer and plan on using this source extensively to earn passive income, you can also start a blog and website to promote your work. And, if you want to do all your own marketing and fulfillment, you'll keep almost 100% of the profits. Of course, it means more time invested, so weigh all the pros and cons of doing so. The beauty of having Amazon handle everything for you is that you won't have to keep accounts, manage payments, handle distribution, refunds, or returns. You should be able to rely on the platforms you use to provide excellent service. They should also have such a huge market, that it makes the job of promoting your books much easier because you will have a broad base of customers. That's why you pay them 30% of your profits.

With all these resources and tools, all you do is come up with exciting and interesting topics. Try to write about topics that are popular, reach a broad customer base, and that aren't already flooding the market. Although that won't even be a concern if your e-Books contain exceptional information and are well written.

Creating an App as Passive Income

Just like the writing process, you don't have to become a professional coder or programmer to create an incredible app. All the development can be done at an affordable price by the experts. Of course, if you want to take the time to learn to code, you can, but this is time spent that could be better used developing more sources of passive income, don't you think? If you are excited about being the idea man or woman and leaving the labor to those who know how to provide you with an incredible product, then let's move forward, shall we?

One of the most frequently asked questions most people have when developing their first app is—how do I know what kind of app to create? Where do I begin? Here are five easy steps to follow that will help you to decide.

1.   Consider a skill or talent you have in which you and others believe to be your particular area of expertise. Perhaps it is a past career, a hobby, or a creative outlet in which you excel. If you can think of nothing you have done where you stood out from the crowd, then think of something that is fascinating to you and perhaps will also be to a wide range of other people.

2.   As you consider your area of expertise, think about a specific problem you had when you were first learning to perform this skill or job. For example, let's say you love to garden and have a talent for growing beautiful vegetables—but, this has not always been the case. Let's say it took you a long time to learn about what soil, seasons, temperatures and sunlight requirements were needed for the many vegetables you were

interested in cultivating. Through many trials and errors, much research and failed attempts, you finally have a productive vegetable garden that consistently raises bumper crops. You could design a handy app to resolve the initial issues that you experienced, so that consumers would only be a click away in determining what vegetable to plant where, when.

3. Now that you have thought of what you want your app to be about ask yourself how you can create an that app to resolve some of the problems you first experienced. How can you help consumers to achieve greater success investing less time and money?

4. Don't rely entirely on yourself when identifying a problem and solution, especially if you are not an expert in your field of interest. Find people who are currently working in your area of interest or enjoying your hobby and ask lots of

questions. Then interview experts to see how they suggest these issues could be resolved. Now, you have the makings of an app.

5.   If you simply cannot think of anything, identify some of the day-to-day, repetitive tasks people do that could be achieved more efficiently if they could just click for information. Apps typically provide excellent solutions for repetitive tasks that many people do on a daily basis.

Now you need to focus on how you plan to market and sell your app. Like e-Books, you can sell your app over the Internet by using platforms such as www.e-junkie or www.gumroad.com. Or, you can sell your app on a third-party marketplace like Win 8App Store or Mac App Store. The advantages of using Microsoft or Apple is that they have massive search engines and amazing delivery systems in place. The only way anybody makes money is when your app sells, so everybody works hard to make sure your app is a success (3).

Similar to Amazon for your e-Books, Apple takes about a 30% cut to bring your app to the consumer. They have certain guidelines you must go through for approval, and, of course, there are many apps available, so the competition is high. However, many app developers have not done near the homework or have near the expertise to back up the function of their apps, right? All the support and visibility Apple can provide will more than makes up for the 30% charge.

Blogging is a Beautiful Thing—Six Steps to Success

Starting a blog doesn't have to be rocket science, but your first time out of the gate can be intimidating, especially if you're not a computer whiz. The following are six easy steps to practice that will help you create an incredible blog and maximize the potential passive income you can generate.

Step #1: Ask yourself why you want to start a blog.

I hope your only answer to this question isn't just to make money. Although it's an excellent way to create passive income, if money is your only reason, you're setting yourself up for failure. Blogs that are started because someone wants to make a difference, to become a better person, or to get published, are going to be ones that attract a bigger following. Unless you are blogging about ways to increase your income—like generating passive income—talking about income made from your blog won't be terribly impressive.

Step #2: What will be the focus of your blog?

What are your hobbies, talents, and things in which you are passionate? When you're with a group of people, what do you find yourself talking about most of the time? That may be your first blog. Make sure the topic of your blog is broad enough to continue sharing information about it over an extended period.

Step #3: What blogging platforms do you plan to use?

There are many free hosting sites; however, since your blog is to promote whatever will create passive income for you, it is better to have a self-hosted WordPress blog. Besides, free blog sites aren't ever free because the myriad of limitations they place on you will inhibit your ability to reach maximum followers. What are the costs of a self-hosted blog? With many hosting accounts, you can get a domain name for free. The average fee for an account is approximately $75 for the first year.

Web Hosting Hub is reliable and affordable. They provide excellent customer support with 99.9% server uptime. They offer a free domain name, and their service is quite easy for beginners. They also offer unlimited bandwidth, disk space, and email accounts. If you are not satisfied, Web Hosting Hub offers a 90-day money back guarantee. If you decide blogging is not for you, you can simply cancel your account and ask for a refund.

Step #5: Create Your Blog

Since this is dependent on which host you chooses to use, the best thing to do is search online for the web host you desire and follow their step-by-step guidelines.

Step #6: Start Blogging

If you have chosen a reputable web host, it is as simple as logging in with your username and password and posting your first blog. Decide how often you wish to post a new blog, and let your readers know. Also, link your blog to your website and your e-Books. This will create excellent synergy for the promotion of all your sources of passive income. The best blogs are ones that are fun, informative, fun, creative, fun, theme based—oh, and did I mention fun (4)?

Whichever sources you decide to use, or if you incorporate all of them in your passive income portfolio, make it entertaining for your followers and yourself. If building passive income becomes a chore, you're not going to want to give up your free time and spare money to make it work. So, the best advice that I can give you is to choose sources of passive income that you will enjoy, and you think others will as well.

CHAPTER 3: REAL ESTATE RETURNS

Owning real estate rental property is a long-term investment. Although it is not as liquid as cash in hand or the bank, it can eventually net you quite a return, especially if you have positive cash flow from your rental. There are certain things to keep in mind when investing in rental property, and they are as follows:

10 Tips for Investing in Rental Property

1. The location is everything.

Make sure your location will support the rent amount needed to cover your mortgage. If not, you'll end up with a negative cash flow that will eat into your passive income. No matter how well-maintained the home or apartment building you are purchasing is, it's not going to be consistently rented if the surrounding neighborhood is dangerous or poorly kept—unless, of course, you plan on being a slum lord, and that's a whole other headache.

2.   When investing, don't be shy about asking for the moon in your purchase contract.

The worse that could happen is that the owner will refuse your offer, and then you can counter in hopes of finding the best possible price. Before you begin the negotiations, decide on what your ceiling offer is, and stick to that figure. The price you pay for the property should be well below the appraised value so that you can start as a landlord in an equal position.

Include, in writing, any additional appliances, fans, and window coverings you want to go with the sale. Also, be aware of other costs that will need to be paid upfront, such as HOA transfer fees and appraisal fees. Because these fees must be paid before the property closes, you don't want to get stuck with these out-of-pocket costs should the property not close. A good practice in these situations is to negotiate that the owner pays these costs and closing costs if possible. If the owner insists on splitting these fees, then negotiate that the owner pays up front and be reimbursed as closing. That way, if the property doesn't close, you won't be out the money.

Since you want to invest as little upfront money as possible, negotiate everything that you can to be put into the mortgage. For example, raise the price of the property and have the owner pay for the closing costs; this will enable you to purchase with no upfront closing costs. Your closing costs will be wrapped into your mortgage. Look for properties that have been on the market for some time, since the owners will be more open to negotiating price or perks. NEVER, EVER purchase property without doing a thorough inspection by a paid professional. When repairs need to be made, either have the repairs completed before closing or ask that the owners renegotiate their asking price.

If the property already has a tenant, realize that you will most likely need to give them a 30-day notice or honor the existing lease agreement. Ask the owners to review the existing rental agreement to see what your obligations are regarding the current tenant. Make sure you have also done an excellent job considering what rents are going for in that area, and see how those properties compare with the one you are interested in purchasing.

3.   The best investment isn't always the prettiest property.

Keep in mind; this is to be a rental property—not one in which you are planning to live. Any improvements made should be practical and economical, not necessarily the most expensive and luxurious. It is usually not a good idea to have a lot of extras on a rental, like a pool or fireplace, for instance. They create additional liabilities, and the cost of maintenance or upkeep cannot be recouped in rental fees.

4.   Be prepared for repairs after each vacating tenant.

Tenants are going to damage your property, and you need to be prepared, so you are not blindsided by costly repairs. It's important that you require regular inspections of the property, done by yourself or your management company. If you see that the property is neglected or abused, give your tenant immediate notice to vacate before you lose money and valuable time making unnecessary repairs. Even though having a management company will cost you a little money upfront, they can save you so much in the long run. Not only will they save you money, but if you actually want passive income from your rentals, then you need to distance yourself from the day-to-day hassles of rental management.

5.   Increase rental incomes for long-term tenants.

The mistake many investors make is that they fail to raise rents for long-term tenants. Your leases should have potential built-in rate increases that are written into the lease agreements. If you have an excellent tenant, then you'll want to reward them by maintaining a reasonable rental fee. However, that doesn't mean never raising the rent. If your tenant has been in the property for a long time, you will still be expected to paint and replace flooring from time to time, and your rental fees will need to cover those costs. Set aside enough positive cash flow to cover repairs and updates to your rental. This will keep it market fresh and make it more appealing to a wide range of potential tenants.

6. Plan on regular tax increases and elevated HOA fees.

Before purchasing your property review what the taxes and HOA fees have done over the past five years. Were the taxes steady, or have they increased substantially? Look at the amount they have increased over this period, and plan on that continuing. The same can be said for HOA fees. First of all, make sure you have included HOA fees in your rental fees because you will be responsible for paying them—not the tenant. You don't want to have taxes and HOA fees eat up your passive income from the property, so those costs should be figured into your rentals.

7. Keep as much money in your pocket as possible.

There are many ways to purchase property that won't cost you an arm and a leg for a down payment and closing costs. In fact, you can buy cooperatively with other investors for as little as $5,000, and enjoy all the benefits of passive income in your rental. If you decide on this method of investing in real estate, make sure you have spelled out in your agreement the requirements of selling your portion of the property. The downside to these types of investments is that it can often be harder to sell your ownership share.

If you decided that shared real estate investment is a way for you to get your foot in the door, one such company to check into is RealtyShares. RealtyShares is one of the largest real estate crowdsourcing companies, and it is based in San Francisco. They include a variety of nationwide investment opportunities in both residential and commercial properties. This can be quite advantageous as you can pick and choose locations around the country, purchasing when the markets are at their best (5).

8.   Don't outstay your welcome in a rental investment.

What I mean by that is that every property has a predetermined useful life. Don't keep the property beyond its earning potential. If the repairs you are consistently making outweigh the return, it may be time to sell and reinvest in another rental. Track your appreciation to determine whether your money would earn you more in a different area of property. In most markets and locations, the life of a property is, at its maximum, no longer than 29 years. The life of a property is dependent upon its age at purchase, and whether it is residential or commercial. Some commercial property has a longer life than residential.

9.   You can also trade properties of like type and value.

There are tax requirements to consider when trading properties, and a professional can help you with this. However, this can be an excellent way to gain instant equity in a property, since the trade does not have term requirements, but only refers to the purchase price. For example, if you have a property that has no equity but is in a great location, and you want cash to invest in additional passive income opportunities, you could trade with someone who does have equity. After the trade, you could then pull some of the equity from your newly acquired property to invest in several others without any out-of-pocket costs.

10. You can also purchase paper (privately held notes or deeds) on a property.

This usually requires more money, but there is no maintenance or upkeep—you are only purchasing the paper. You don't own the property, unless, of course, the payee should default—which would mean you own the entire property for a fraction of the price. When you purchase paper, you own the paper or the loan. For example, let's say the original owner sold the home that he owned free and clear and created a private mortgage or loan on the property for the buyers. Each month, the buyer makes a payment of $1,000 to the original owner. Because the original owner was willing to carry the financing, he receives significantly more interest on his money—let's say 10%. The remainder owed on the loan is $50,000 at 10% interest.

For personal reasons, the original owner decides he needs cash and wants to sell the private note he is carrying at a substantial discount. It is feasible that you could purchase a $50,000 note for $30,000 and make 10% interest on your investment. You will still have to honor the terms of the original loan, but you have just made $20,000, and you will earn a good deal more money on your investment. Of course, you too have the option to sell the paper to another investor like yourself who is also interested in purchasing the paper.

Don't worry about the chances of the buyers defaulting because that is not a bad thing for your investment. If they default, then you are the owner of the property. The more equity in the property, the better. In fact, a good rule of thumb when investing in the paper is that there should be at least 10% equity in the property. More equity is always better, but 10% equity is a must.

There are so many different opportunities to make passive income in real estate investments; whatever you can imagine can usually be created in a purchase agreement. Just be careful that you have done your homework and that you are not buying something with an inflated price or unreasonable terms. If you find that real estate is your primary source of passive income, you may want to consider obtaining a real estate license so you can save yourself the commissions on the property you sell and get paid the commissions on ones you purchase. That's a whole other source of passive income. It doesn't require any more work than your original purchase, and you'll be putting commissions in your pocket.

CHAPTER 4: INVESTING IN STOCKS, BONDS & ANNUITIES

Investing in stocks, bonds, and annuities can mean a chunk of change, so you may want to start out smaller and work your way up to this type of passive income. Let your money work for you on your other ventures and then use those profits to invest in stocks, bonds, and annuities. You can also make interest off CDs held in the bank, but today's rates are so low it won't gain you much income. There are different ways to invest in stocks, but if you are unfamiliar with the market the best way is to hire a reputable broker.

The safest way to invest your money is to do so with stable, reliable companies. Your returns won't be huge, but, as I said before, passive income is not a get-rich-quick scheme. You've got time, so it's probably better to play it safe and let your passive income gradually build. Of course, you're not always going to come out a winner, so if you're the anxious type who watches his or her money fluctuate each day and gets stressed with the roller-coaster ride of trading stocks, then this is not the best option for you.

If you decide to give it a try, develop a relationship with a good broker. Communicate your goals to your broker and trust them to help you choose which stocks to invest in and what is better left to the high-risk players. There are also stock options you can consider, but those are beyond the scope of this book. It will take some research for you to decide which stock to purchase and how many shares. If you are interested, the best thing is to research, study the market for a while before investing, and then pick a few favorites to watch for a while before you lay down the cash.

Diversify your stocks so that if one is down perhaps the others will be on the rise. Don't invest more than you can afford to lose. Investing in dividend-bearing stocks is an excellent way to periodically draw money on your investment without selling the stock. Choosing stable, reliable companies will enable you to collect regularly paid dividends and still leave your investment and let it continue to create more passive income. By choosing well, diversifying your portfolio, and investing several thousand dollars in dividend-based stock, you stand to make four to five percent on your investment without selling. It's passive but, don't kid yourself; it can be quite stressful.

If you're planning the DIY type of stock investing, let us warn you that the learning curve can be very expensive. Years ago, a close friend of my family decided to spend her $35,000 inheritance in the stock market. She thought it would be fun to become a day trader and work from home, and felt her inheritance would give her a good start. She read up and studied the market for months before finally quitting her job and buying her stock. Within a matter of six months, she had lost all her money and was out looking for another job. Although day trading can sound like a lot of fun, it requires knowledge and nerves of steel to hang in there through the ups and downs of the market.

One of the best investments for a novice trader is Exchange-Traded

Funds (ETFs). These are investments that have assets such as stocks,

bonds, and commodities; however, they are easier to understand and

much more liquid. They also come with a lower price tag than

investing in mutual funds. ETFs are especially rewarding for the

young investor who doesn't have much money to spend so he or she

would be unable to make a broker's deposit of $5,000 to $10,000, but

they would enjoy a higher-risk stock. ETFs could either be included

in their portfolio, or the trader could invest in ETFs entirely. It is still

required, however, to pay a broker's fee on every ETF transaction (6).

Investing in Bonds and Bank Savings

These are probably the safest investment, and yet your gains will be

minimal. If you have waited until you are retired to begin building

passive income, these are not going to mature quickly enough to

make a difference. They are such a solid investment, and you can

count on them to grow to match inflation, but not much more. The

biggest risk made when investing in bonds is that you have left

money on the table by not putting your money somewhere else that could have grown faster and significantly increased your passive income.

There are short-term and long-term bonds with differing maturity dates. Think of bonds like a loan and the maturity date as the time in which the bond issuer is required to pay you back the entire loan amount. The longer the term to maturity, the more time you'll have to collect interest on the bond. The benefit to you for lending the money is that you get to collect interest on the bond, and at the time of maturity you get back your initial investment. The only time you would not get your investment back is if the issuer has defaulted or you sell the bond to another investor before its maturity.

If you want to avoid broker fees, you can purchase bonds directly from the Treasure. Just visit their online site at http://www.treasurydirect.gov and everything will be handled electronically. If you are using a broker and have decided to include bonds in your portfolio, you will then pay a broker's fee. Most brokers will ask for a minimum deposit of $5,000 to $10,000 to open your account and invest your money, so be prepared (7).

Bank CDs are less of a risk than bonds, but they also provide fewer returns. The beauty of CDs is that they are liquid (easily converted to cash) should you need your money in a hurry. The problem with CDs in today's market is their interest is so low, your money is better spent in another passive source. The interest on a CD depends on how much you put into the CD and how long you plan to leave it there. You can put thousands into a CD and commit to leaving it there for years and still get no more than 1 or 2 percent return. No risk—no return. It would probably cost you more in gas to pick up your money.

Investing in Annuities

Annuities are typically purchased from an insurance company. You buy the policy and then it pays you a specified amount each year for the rest of your life. The younger you are when you invest in the annuity, the less it will pay you each year. The dangers with annuities are that the insurance company might go belly-up and leave you holding the bag. For this reason, choose insurance companies that have been around for years and have proven themselves in the marketplace. You also may wish to diversify when investing in annuities, spreading your money with several insurance companies.

Annuities can also be inherited, but make sure you communicate to your beneficiary any annuity you may have. Insurance companies are not held liable to inform recipients that their deceased donor had an annuity that was willed to them and they are now the recipient of thousands of dollars. Don't hold your breath on that happening! If your chosen beneficiary doesn't know to call and notify the insurance company of the change in name or status of the annuity, they might not ever collect. By the time your intended beneficiary got around to discovering you willed your annuity to them, the insurance company may well have eaten up the profits in service fees (8).

If you are a bit intimidated with the thought of investing in stocks and annuities, that's understandable. Starting small is difficult with these types of investments, especially if your broker requires large deposits. Some brokerage houses will allow novice investors to begin with minimum deposits of a few thousand dollars, and some offer you investment money to sign up with their investment firm. A word of caution, be careful when going with brokers who entice with free offers. There might be a good reason they feel as though they must pay for their clients.

Investing in the market is not for the faint of heart. So, if you don't do stress—don't invest, especially if you are investing money that you would lose sleep over if you lost it tomorrow. Stick to other ways to create passive income that won't give you heartburn if you should drop a few thousand during your learning curve. For some, that could be all the money they have saved or earned by their entire stream of passive income. Don't risk it all—instead, start small!

CHAPTER 5: BUILDING/BUYING WEBSITES & DOMAINS

There is a whole new world of online commerce out there in the form of websites and domains. You can build them, buy them, or flip them, but whatever you do will mean some upfront investment of time and money. Of course, you can always think of a domain name, register it, and use or sell it. You can do the same with a website— build it or pay for it to be built, then use it to promote your stream of passive income. Sounds good, but those of you who have ever attempted to have experts create a website for you know the expense and frustration that can cause. The DIY job of building a website doesn't get you the optimization you'll need to put your business on the map. So, what do you do?

The first website I built was through GoDaddy. While it looked good, it was not successful at driving browsers to my site. I knew nothing of keywords, WordPress, reviews, ads, links, nothing—and so that is what the website was worth to my business—absolutely nothing. Then I met with an SEO and paid to have the website optimized. Eight-hundred dollars later, I still had an attractive website, and I believed the SEO was working on my behalf to make the site more functional, but, to tell you the truth, after months of asking where we were at with the optimization, I still had a whole lot of nothing. No more responses, very little traffic, and an empty purse.

Next, I hired a professional design company to give me a fresh start and create a whole new website for my business. This time I paid $16,000, and it looked outstanding. It was highly functioning, did exactly what I wanted it to do, drove business to the site, but there was one problem. I could not maintain the site myself. About once a week I had a challenge on the site that needed attention, and there I was—dependent upon the web designers to change the code and make the site work more efficiently. So now, not only was it highly expensive, it was extremely time-consuming. I ended up selling the business after 18 months. It was profitable and the woman who purchased my business also owns the website. It was still a startup with existing contracts of over $60,000. The company sold for $32,000, which was barely enough to cover my cost of developing and maintaining the website during those miserable 18 months.

Who reaped the benefits of my website business? The person who purchased it; she didn't have to go through the months of frustrating design and content development or the initial start-up hassles for website maintenance and support. Since this was years ago, I didn't know about website sales, and they might not have even existed back then. I didn't sell my site, I sold my business. The problem was, I didn't think of my website as my business; I thought of it as a way to market my business.

The reason I share this story is that I wanted to give you a better perspective on how to think of a website. When I refer to selling websites, what I'm talking about is selling businesses. There are many sites online that have listings of website businesses for sale.

They range from $50 on up to $15,000 or more. Sometimes the better bargain is not to build your site from scratch, but to buy a bargain business and let it provide immediate passive income.

There will always be the high-priced website companies that you pass by because you think they are cost prohibitive, but stop for a moment and give it a second look. If it is already making a sizeable passive income, you may want to take on a partner and do a little coop investing. Then there are the budget website businesses that you, again, pass by because you believe they couldn't be worth the hosting fees, right? Not necessarily. Look again. If the website is of interest to you, examine it to see how you could ramp up the site and generate new business. If all you save is the cost of website design, that, in itself, could mean thousands of dollars in your pocket.

Then there are the website businesses that are not too flashy, but they consistently perform. For most of you first-time website buyers, this will be the place to start to build up your site passive income (9). If your talent lies in writing code or programming, what are you thinking? Start building businesses around a website and then sell it, for goodness sake! Or, partner with a content writer, and together create some unusual sources for making passive income.

A real inexpensive way to build passive income is by buying domain names. They are inexpensive and, if you've done your homework, can be sold for incredible profits. Let me give you five easy to remember tips on what not to do when you're planning to buy and sell domain names.

5 Easy Tips on What Not to Do When Buying Domains

1. Don't cruise lots of sites looking for domain names, or versions of the domain names you like, to see if they are taken. Decide where you want to purchase your domain, and stick to that sight. Most domain names cost $10. If you find the domain is available, buy it immediately. Don't wait until

after dinner because, if it's a hot name that just happened to become available, it will be taken by then.

2.   Don't ask other people what they think of your domain name. It might give them the idea to buy it before you and then sell back to you for a profit.

3.   Don't buy just one version of the same domain. They are only $10, buy up the .net, .com, .org, .biz, all of them. What do you think another who likes your name will do when they see the domain is taken and not for sale? They will usually go to another version of the same name. For example, if .com is taken, they'll choose .net. If you own all the versions of the same domain, you can sell the .com version to them for a sizeable profit.

4.   Don't buy a lot of domain names that you just think are cool. Look to see what the latest trends are in business. New business start-ups are public record, and corporations must

publish their openings in the paper. Search to find what types of businesses are popular and then put yourself in the place of the owner. What names might relate to those kinds of businesses? Then, simply buy the domains.

5.   Don't feel like you can't ask for a lot of money because you only paid $10 for the domain. Many rookie business owners fail to set up their businesses correctly, and that includes registering their names. By the time they get around to doing so, their preferred name is taken, and they are then required to pay much, much more for the domain name. You were the visionary, and you should reap the benefits.

Finding places to buy and sell websites and domains are just a matter of a little online research. Many sites will lead you to these wonderful little gold mines of passive income.

CHAPTER 6: MONITOR & ADJUST YOUR SOURCES

Even though all these sources for passive income eventually take very little time, you still need to monitor the results of your investments and make the necessary adjustments for them to continue to run smoothly. If you're writing eBooks and creating apps, you need to keep your pipeline filled with current books and apps continually. If you are purchasing a rental property, you'll need to continuously search the market for bargains and determine which of your current assets are ready to be sold. If you are buying and selling websites and domains, it's a constant search for good little businesses and names. Think of yourself as the CEO of your passive income business. You don't have to do the grunt labor, just show up now and then.

Now you know why I said in the very beginning that it takes a lot of creativity and innovative thinking to create viable passive income. Don't turn this endeavor into a job, keep it adventurous. This is your chance to be an entrepreneur, to discover all the many ways or different businesses you can create that take little to no startup cost with a minimal amount of time spent in maintaining their ongoing profits.

I will tell you; it will be quite tempting to spend your passive income when you see it begin to roll in, but resist. Celebrate just a little, briefly indulge yourself, then set aside some money for more investments and always save. I've found that when you have passive income and things get tough, everything comes crashing down at once. It can be very discouraging, and many who made a good start on building passive income quit during the first storm because they weren't prepared to ride it out—both financially and emotionally.

By monitoring and adjusting what works and what doesn't work, your stream will stay active and your passive income consistent. Frequently examine the cost, in time and money, to maintain your sources of passive income. If one source of passive income costs you more time than you want to devote to it, drop it. That's not failing; it's called smart business practices. Some sources you don't have to drop; just let them ride away into the sunset until they dry up and stop producing altogether. However, there are other things you will need to shut down, or the small strings of business will make you crazy to maintain them. It will be too much work for too little returns.

Always search for new sources of passive income. What you think are great sources today will become obsolete tomorrow. It's an ever-changing ocean of newness; to be most successful you must surf the curl or be buried by the waves of change. Stay current with technology, and learn how to make it work for you. Technology an excellent tool, even if used only to track your successes and setbacks. Make technology your business partner; in doing so, you can often create new business in a matter of days and change existing ones at the click of a key.

This doesn't have to be a business of one. In some of my businesses, I've taken on partners who were more technically savvy than me, or who were experts in the field in which I wished to learn more. That doesn't mean you should partner in every source of your passive income, but in some avenues having a partner enables you to make more money in less time. If you do take on a partner, make sure you have clearly communicated your expectations and put everything in writing.

Most importantly, and I cannot emphasize this enough, make it FUN! Build passive income by doing the things you've always wanted to do, by creating unique and entertaining profitable avenues of revenue. It is so much easier to market businesses that you believe in and enjoy. It's just natural to want to talk to your friends about what you're doing when you love your work.

I've heard it said that work should fund your life but not be your life. I'm not so sure this is the case with passive income. What you enjoy most in life soon becomes the work that you enjoy most. I love my work so much; it's difficult for me to separate the two at times. I can't imagine going on vacation and not thinking about what my sources of passive income are doing while I'm away. Most people think of their pets having a field day while they are away, but those of us who love creating passive income have better things on which to focus. We know the importance of keeping our creative juices flowing all the time. Think of your passive income as a game—a game where you get to make the rules and determine the outcomes.

Be prepared for some ups and downs, especially when you first begin building your stream. If you're going to ride the rapids, you'll have to learn to navigate the rocky patches without drowning. It's an important time to share with a loved one or close friend what you are planning to do—someone who will encourage you—someone with whom you can celebrate your successes. Choose these people carefully because in the beginning stage of your new passive income career, they may be the determining factor of whether you hang in there or drop out. Good luck with your efforts. Keep me posted; I'll love to share in all your victories.

PART 3

Chapter 1: Create an eBook Empire

Well yes, the truth is – people are loving eBooks. A comprehensive 2012 survey by Pew Research Center discovered that about 43 percent of Americans read a book or long content (journals, magazines etc.) on an electronic device. The survey also revealed about 28 percent Americans owned a minimum of one electronic reading device. You can only imagine how much the numbers would have grown since. Packed with practicality (well, even the biggest home library may not be able to accommodate a million books), portability and quick access, eBooks are transforming the way people read. Why not cash in on this wonderful development and create some useful, information-packed and interesting books that will add value to people's lives? Here's all the meat and juice for creating your own successful eBook empire.

Find a Passion

We all have that one thing which lights the fire in us. What is that one topic or niche which you can talk on or write about for hours?

Fitness? Psychic powers? Cooking? Raising children? Write down a list of possible ideas you can think of which you see yourself writing with knowledge and passion. Build mind maps once you've decided on the core topic. These can include all the sub topics you may want to include within the main topic. For instance, if you are putting together a fitness related eBook, think of all the chapters/sub topics/sub niches to be included in it.

This can be fitness workouts, diets to complement your workouts, ideal fitness attire, fitness gear, fitness stretches and the likes. Similarly, if you find the marketplace is already crowded with too many fitness related books, you can narrow down your focus to a single aspect of fitness. Say Post Pregnancy Fitness – How to Get Back in Shape After Having a Baby. If you are already an expert in a specific niche, such as a child psychologist or real estate attorney or wedding planner, jump right in within your area of expertise.

Start Writing

Once you have a topic in place, begin a rough table of contents draft for the book. This will help you flesh out the topics later. You can use any word processor such as Notepad or Word. Some people prefer Evernote. If you are not comfortable writing it as a single document, break down the documents chapter-wise. This way you can move around and access various chapters quickly and then put them together in the end.

You will have to play around with images, font sizes, colors and headers to make huge chunks of text easy to read. Make the book look interesting, easy on the eye and navigation friendly. In the end, put all the chapters together to create a seamless flow.

Convert It into an eBook

A simple Google search should give you multiple options for converting a word document into an eBook. You simply need to upload a word file and it is converted into an eBook. Calibre is a free software that can be downloaded and used for word processor to eBook conversion. Go through everything to ensure the formatting is in place. If you are using Amazon Kindle Publishing (inarguably the best platform for eBook greenhorns), there's a preview tool that lets you see a final version of the book so you know exactly how the formatting will appear on electronic devices.

Create A Stunning Cover

You can create a gorgeous looking eBook cover using either some type of graphic software program such as Photoshop or Ms Office (Powerpoint, Word etc). You can also hire the services of expert graphic designers on freelance project sites. Look at other covers for inspiration. Get a feel of them on the Kindle eBook store. Once you have a design and layout in mind, create and upload it. Amazon also has a handy cover creator, which can be used for building quick and effective eBook covers. Amazon will only display your book cover in the "Customers Who Bought This Item Also Bought" to trigger reader curiosity. Ensure that it is sharp, attention-grabbing and relevant.

Pricing Your eBook

Amazon gives you the option of picking your own book pricing plan. You can either avail 35 percent profits by setting your own price or 70 percent profits by pricing your book according to Amazon's prescribed price between $2.99 to $9.99. Unless there is a strong business plan behind pricing your book outside $2.99 to$ 9.99, it makes sense to keep a major chunk of your profits.

Promote The Book Extensively

Amazon will only boost your sale and reach when you fulfill the requirement of their complex algorithms. You will have to promote and push your book initially to get support from them. This can be done by creating a few high quality guest blog posts on sites/blogs related to your book. You can include a snippet about the book in the author bio to pique the interest of readers. Another great way is to take interesting and meaningful lines from your book and convert them into quote memes or tweets. Lots of people sharing and re-tweeting them will help you garner a large audience. Include a link to your book wherever permissible. Social media updates, blogs, email signatures and the likes.

A good way to build a bank of reviews and customers is to distribute free copies to people within your social network and ask them for genuine reviews. You can also price the book at a discounted rate in the early launch stages and ask the first few buyers to write reviews, before changing to the regular price. It always helps to have some reviews in there when readers are trying to make purchase related choices.

Another advantage of having a lot of early buyers is that Amazon boosts popular titles and gives it even more exposure once they see a lot of people picking it up. This can massively help your rankings.

Other Publishing Channels

Other than Kindle Publishing, you can also publish your book on your own website. It may not enjoy a roaring exposure initially or at least not as much as large platform like Amazon, however over a period of time, you can enjoy higher profits. Third party hosting merchants may charge you a small percentage fee of about 1 to 5 percent for accepting customer payments and delivering the content to them in a downloadable format.

Chapter 2: Creating Killer Blogs

Blog– the internet marketer's golden word. And rightly so. Imagine creating a single valuable, detailed, comprehensive and well-researched post just once and earning from it years after you have published it. Blogs can be used in tandem with other passive income sources such as membership based training programs or eBooks. They can also be stand-alone income generators. You can earn revenue through advertising programs such as Google Adsense. Then there's the highly lucrative world of affiliate marketing and list building. Selling banner advertisements, physical products, courses, eBooks and more is just the tip of the ice-berg. There is really so much you can do with an informative, valuable and content-packed blog.

Pack Value Which is Tough To Find Elsewhere

Pick a topic you are passionate about and know well. Do not simply trend hop and know what topics are popular. Yes, you need to do basic keyword research to determine if there's sufficient demand for your niche but don't obsess too much about finding the most populated niches. The challenge is to grab any niche you like and make it popular! Go with specific topics or sub niches to laser target your audience and gain monopoly within the sub niche. For instance, if you find that weight loss is an overcrowded niche, try dominating a sub-niche such as post pregnancy weigh loss or weight loss for seniors. This way you get a more focused audience, who you can sell and market to, with comparatively lesser competition.

Create Interesting and Valuable Content

Create original, engaging, unique and useful content that gives your readers more value. Explore your expertise and write about something that you have a good knowledge or background of. Use powerful elements to support your text such as images, videos and infographics. Use screenshots wherever required to make the content clearer for your target audience. This will require more time and effort than a simple text blog, however it will help your search engine rankings and will give you lots of loyal readers.

Choose A Blogging Platform

If you are serious about starting a blog that generates passive income, avoid using a free blogging platform and opt for the WordPress self-hosted medium. WordPress is one of the most widely used, customizable, easy to operate and visually stunning blogging platforms. The self-hosted option allows you to set up banner advertisements and use affiliate market links within the blog. Your blog URL looks more professional, in addition to the fact that you will be able to play with abundant features for beautifying your blog. Find a reliable hosting service and a brandable, memorable and unique domain name.

Blog Interface

If content is the king, your blog design is the queen. It will determine many factors such as the stickiness of your blog, the time people spend on your blog, the click through rate of your links and much more. Opt for a clean, well-defined and user friendly interface. Use can either use a WordPress theme or buy them from a third party like Themeforest.net. You can also pick between free and paid themes. Paid themes add more bells and whistles to your blog to make it look attention grabbing and professional. Themes can be changed instantly by going to the Appearances section of your WordPress admin panel. Ensure you pick a responsive theme for your blog as a majority of users access the internet from hand held devices.

Make it easy for visitors to find everything on your blog by organizing all relevant tabs on your home page. Balance colors well, and leave enough white space to give the eye some relief. Use customized headers created by a professional graphic artist. Improve the readability of your blog by using subheads, bullets, text bubbles for important text, tables, charts, illustrations and more. This helps attention starved people pick key points from your content without having to go through the entire piece.

Monetizing The Blog

Advertising Program – You can 'rent' out space on your site to popular advertising programs such as Google Adsense, Yahoo Bing Network, Clicksor and more. These ad networks keep the advertisements relevant to your blog content and pay you a small amount every time a visitor on your site clicks on the advertisement. The best part is you aren't creating or selling any products but simply using the space on your blog to create passive income.

Affiliate Marketing – Affiliate marketing is all about selling other people's products on your site and earning a commission on every sale or lead that is fulfilled through a link on your blog. Say for instance, you run a pet travel site and have a steady stream of pet owners who travel with their pets. You can sign up as an affiliate for a puppy discipline informational eBook or a nationwide network of pet care and grooming services. So each time a pet owner buys the book or signs up for the pet grooming services, you get a nice little commission. Though individual products and services may have their own affiliate program, some popular marketplaces where you can find several affiliate programs are Clickbank, Offervault, Markethealth, ShareASale, Commission Junction and Avangate.

1. Review Writing – Writing useful, comprehensive and well-researched reviews is one of the best ways to sink your teeth into the world of affiliate marketing. Indentify high quality products with top-notch customer support, which can be really useful for your audience. Draft lengthy reviews to promote the products (include both pros and cons) and make your buyer's decision making process simpler. Reviews are often sought by people who are already half way within the buying cycle (with some options at hand) and giving them

a good overview of the product will help you complete the sale.

2. Promote The Right Products – This should be fairly obvious yet it is surprising how many folks get it all wrong when it comes to promoting the right products. Find products that feature high ratings, superior quality, decent recommendations and most important – are relevant for your audience. Promoting dubious products and scams spell doom for affiliate marketers. You might make those first few sales by luring people, however your long term credibility may take a massive blow. If you plan to stick around for long and build a dependable source of passive income, pick your products judiciously.

3. Think Out Of The Box – If you believe the virtual world is already choc-o-bloc with multiple affiliate offers, think out of the box and act as an affiliate for local businesses. Use conventional businesses to generate profitable commissions. For example, let us assume you run an interior design and decorator blog that gives people interesting home makeover ideas. You can tie up with home improvement companies, contractors and furniture suppliers in your neighborhood for lead capturing or selling their products to your readers. You may also be running a city or region based blog, and promoting local

businesses may be the perfect passive income business model.

4. Diversify – Diversify your affiliate marketing offers, yet do not crowd your blog with too many sales pitches. Pick a handful of good offers and start promoting them. For example, for a travel blog, you can promote multiple products/programs such as backpacks, a traveler blogger training program, photography equipment and more. This way you are catering to diverse needs and pulling in bigger profits.

5. Links – Use link cloakers to get rid of the ugly, long and unprofessional looking affiliate links. They make your links appear cleaner, shorter and more professional, while also boosting your click-through figures. Another pro tip is to make the visuals on your blog clickable. When images are made clickable by linking back to the sales page of the offer you are promoting, enthusiastic customers are immediately led to the relevant buying page. When you are eagerly looking to buy something or thinking about buying something, you don't want a tacky looking image upload page to play mood killer. User experience is a huge factor in determining the success of your affiliate marketing blog.

6. Selling Banner Ads – Once your blog attains considerable popularity, you can consider selling banner ad spaces to businesses related to your blog. You have complete control over how much you charge these businesses since you are directly dealing with them. If you draw impressive traffic figures from a well-targeted audience, companies will be willing to negotiate lucrative advertising revenue.

7. Selling Informational Products – Selling your own digital products is another source of passive income. These can eBooks, short reports, email courses or membership programs. If you have high-quality, original and problem-solving content on your blogs, you will build a loyal base of readers who trust your expertise. They will be more than happy to buy informational products from you. The book can be sold to your mail subscribers or directly on your blog/website using an attention-grabbing landing page. You can also put the book for sale on the Amazon Kindle Publishing platform.

8. Directory Listings – When your blog becomes fairly, you can start a paid listings section and rake in a good amount of income from it. The services can be related to your blog content. For instance, if you are running a blog related to wedding planning, and pull in a huge

traffic of soon to be brides, you can put up listings of professionals offering wedding related services such as florists, bakers, decorators, jewelers and travel companies. This helps to add an extra income avenue to your blog. Passive income is all about diversifying and optimizing income from a single source.

9. Pay Per Lead For Local Businesses – Imagine you have a thriving blog that focuses on real estate and attracts lots of real estate buyers and sellers who are hungry for information. How about working out an arrangement with local real estate firms/professionals to pay you per buyer/seller lead you send them? Leads can be captured by informing your audience that you can help them find some of the best properties in their area. It is a win-win situation for all. Again, passive income is thinking out of the box and leveraging multiple income streams to maximize your profits.

10. Promotions and Paid Recommendations/Reviews – Once you gain considerable authority in your niche and are often referred to as an industry influencer, you can easily do paid reviews/recommendations or draft promotional posts. At this stage, you will most likely have a large following of people who trust your

opinion. Cash in on it by promoting others' products and services through promotional posts. Make sure that you don't fill your blog solely with promotional posts and maintain a fine balance between promotional and non-promotional content. The idea is not merely to sell to your target audience, but to help them buy by recommending really great stuff which makes their life simpler.

11. List Building – A blog that attracts a steady stream of targeted visitors can be great for list building. Place a sign-up box prominently on your blog to attract a swarm of organic subscribers from well-targeted traffic. These are a bunch of already interested action takers, and you could sell just about any related offers, programs, courses, services and products to them. When people sign up for a mailing list, they are voluntarily expressing their interest in knowing more about the products/services being promoted by you. These leads can be used to generate a decent amount of passive income by boosting your sales conversions.

To get potential customers to sign up for your list, make them an offer they can't refuse. Throw in a free eBook or offer them a 10-15 day course. You can also include your affiliate links within the eBook or course. For example, if you are offering an eBook that offers WordPress site creation to beginners, you may want to suggest a good domain name registration and hosting service. Sign up as an affiliate of a reputed web hosting and domain name service and recommend it to your buyers in the course of the book.

Chapter 3: Create Your Own You Tube Channel

Did you know that You Tube has 60 hours of video uploaded on it every 60 seconds? Or that more than 4 billion videos are watched every day? The platform gets a crazy 800 million unique visitors every month (source – Jeffbullas.com). There is a marked shift from consuming text related content to content that is more interactive and real time. Users with low attention spans find it way more convenient to see something than read about it. Also, the demand for video based content is at an all time high, with lesser competition than text based blogs. Not many people are confident about facing the camera, and that's where you can cash in while the space is relatively less crowded.

Belonging To The Big G Family Helps

Since You Tube comes from the Google stable, it is hugely favored by the big G in their organic search results. If you optimize your video for search engines by using the right keywords in the title, meta tags and descriptions, your videos will enjoy higher placement rankings in search results. It is much easier to get a You Tube video to rank on Google compared to a blog post.

Go With Technical and Problem Solving Topics

The nature of You Tube fits very well with technical and problem solving topics where people are looking for very specific solutions. For instance, someone may want to know how to create a table of contents on MS Word or the basics of using MS Excel. Isn't it easier to get a step by step demonstration of using these features rather than simply reading about them? Similarly, cooking, DIY crafts and product demonstrations are extremely popular on You Tube.

When users watch videos on your You Tube channel, there are related ads that pop up on the screen. When visitors click on these ads, you get paid for it. This is why it is emphasized that you have a focused and clear problem solving niche. Comedians or other You Tube performers may not enjoy much ad relevancy since they do not have a very focused audience. However, if you are extremely popular, you may make a considerable income even with low click through rates.

Unconventional ways to approach a conventional topic works wonderfully on You Tube. Throw in a lot of wit, creativity, visual play and humor to illustrate complex topics. Offer interesting metaphors and analogies, and include surprise elements that make your audience take notice.

Use Your Watermark For Videos

Always use a watermark of your blog for your videos. This way users will know exactly where the videos originated from, which will make it easier for them to track your blog and channel. Some users may embed your video on their site. Having a clear watermark with your blog's name can drive more traffic and create a brand identity. Since descriptions only show up on You Tube and not other blogs where your video might be embedded, your URL can be made visible in the watermark.

Start With An Overview

Though videos are easier to watch than elaborate pieces of text, getting a user to watch an entire video is going be a challenge. How do you ensure that users are glued to your videos until the end?

Simple. Just begin with an interesting overview of everything that's included in the video. This whets their appetite and keeps them hooked. This breaks the ice with your user, engages them and boosts their chances of sticking around. Get them interested and enthusiastic about what you are covering in your video. Make an exciting visual summary or map about what's coming up next. Giving them pointers about upcoming content is a great way to make them stay.

Create A Fantastic Call To Action

All your efforts of filming spectacular videos with the best sound and visual effects can be pointless if you do not include a compelling and impactful call to action at the end of it. Including a clear and attention grabbing call to action ensures you don't leave your viewers high and dry after getting them interested with the video. They should know exactly what to do next if they want know more about your products or services. Ask them to visit your website or blog or follow you on various social networks. If they sit through the entire video, they most likely are in a more positive and action oriented state of mind to follow what you tell them to do.

Optimize Your Videos

One solid tip for optimizing your You Tube videos and making them more findable is to include your main keyword in the title followed by a subtitle that lists your secondary keyword and is a rephrased version of the main title. For instance, if you have a video talking about various retirement plans, you can title is as Retirement Saving Plans: 30 Brilliant Tips For Planning a Hassle-Free Retirement.

Also, ensure your video descriptions are keyword optimized, appealing, clear and descriptive. This makes it easy for search engines to place them at the top of relevant searches.

Leverage The Trailer Video Feature

If you want to convert walk-in or browse through viewers into loyal subscribers, utilize You Tube's trailer video feature optimally. The platform allows you to include a video at the top of your channel to give non subscribers a glimpse of your channel. This acts like a teaser to pique your audience's curiosity. Make a powerful, sticky and appealing trailer video to bag more subscribers.

Another super layout tip is to opt for the Player view over Grid View.

Unlike Grid View, Player view sets a single large video on auto-play.

Be Prolific And Upload Frequently

There are no two ways about it. If you are looking to generate passive income from your YouTube channel, you must keep adding content prolifically. The more videos you have out there and the more consistently you post these videos, the higher are your chances of creating a decent income bank. Create an editorial planner and plan to post your videos at regular intervals.

Create and upload videos that talk about different aspects of your niche/topic/industry to build an influential channel. For example, if you run a You Tube channel related to post pregnancy weight loss fitness regimes, try and include other related information such as healthy recipes for new mothers or post pregnancy wardrobe ideas or newborn baby care tips. Try and explore the topic from varied angles so visitors keep coming back for more.

Chapter 4: Sell With Amazon FBA

Dropshipping is another convenient and lucrative online passive income option. A large number of virtual entrepreneurs prefer the dropshipping business model for its flexibility and simplicity. You don't need space to maintain a product inventory. Similarly, there is minimal capital investment in setting up an ecommerce venture. While FBA (Fulfillment By Amazon) requires a flexible product investment, regular dropshopping doesn't need any upfront product investment.

The orders are fulfilled by a retail giant such as Aamzon, while you get to make a neat profit behind every sale. The best part about this business is that you can sell a huge variety of products without having to worry about maintaining a large inventory. There's little wonder that FBA has become one of the most popular home business ventures.

FBA is a super way to leverage the power of Amazon for making profits. You do not have to deal with the sales, buyers or shipping process. Your only job is to source products and send them to

Amazon for maintaining your inventory. Your products receive massive exposure in Amazon's marketplace. They store your product within their network of warehouses and deliver it to your customers. Heck, they even offer customer service. Couldn't be simpler, could it? A great way to rake in passive income, you say? Well yes and no. It is convenient and simple, but not a get rich overnight scheme. You need to invest considerable time and efforts in researching and indentifying products that will sell like hot cakes. You will also need to find suppliers and negotiate prices with them. However, once you are all set, it can't get any more passive than this. You literally don't have to do anything to bring in sales and deliver orders.

Upfront Costs

Unlike dropshipping, you will need a small investment to put together a product inventory for FBA and ship it to Amazon's warehouses. Other than physical product and forwarding charges, expenses you will incur include Amazon's referral fee, subscription fees (either 0.99/transaction or $39.99 monthly plan) and inventory storing fees.

The FBA calculator helps you work a selling price by considering exact fees and shipping charges. Your aim is to find unique products that people need at the right price and price them correctly to maximize your profits. The investment is completely up to the seller. You can buy products worth $10000 or $500. Start small to test your markets and scale up once you see results. Invest as much as you can afford to lose, pick your products carefully and price them judiciously.

If you are just getting your feet wet in FBA or sell more big ticket items in small quantities, you may be better off picking the $0.99/transaction subscription fee option. This plan lets you sell up to 40 products a month. However, if you reckon selling more than 40 products each month, it makes sense to sign up for the $39.99 monthly fee. This is good value for serious folks who plan to carry out hundreds of transactions each month. There are plenty of addition features, such as generating business reports in the latter.

The FBA Edge

What are the benefits of selling on FBA?

FBA items rank higher when people search for specific products.

They also show up frequently on the recommended buy box option, even over items that are priced lower. Buyers are almost always likelier to opt for recommended products.

FBA products are eligible for Amazon Prime membership benefits like complimentary next day delivery, thus making Prime members much more likely to purchase these products.

You get access to an amazing and widely used sales platform, enjoy higher search rankings, and a well-oiled, almost automated system that helps your generate huge profits consistently.

Signing Up For FBA

Start by heading to sellercentral.amazon.com. You can either register for an FBA account with your existing credentials or create a brand new account. Pick your subscription plan depending on the number of products you expect to sell. You can either use your company's legal name or your name. Fill in your credit card number and other details. Credit card details are shared upfront so your account can be charged in the event that you run into a deficit. This can occur when you do not have any sales, yet have to bear warehouse storage and subscription fees.

Next, pick your display name. Remember, this is your brand identity. Make it unique, memorable and likeable. You audience must be able to identify and relate with it. It should be relevant to your niche, if you are focusing on a specific group of products.

You will be required to confirm your identity with a phone call or text message. This completes your registration process. Fill in your bank account details so your earnings can be directly deposited into your account. The deposit method can be selected by going to the Setting tab, and picking an option from the scroll down under Account Info. Verify your bank details to start receiving payments.

At this stage you are an Amazon Seller but not yet registered for FBA. Now, visit the FBA registration page and hit on Get Started to launch your FBA seller account.

Finding the Right Products

To begin with, you will have to be on the look-out for bargains and then measure them up against existing Amazon listings to anticipate how they will perform in comparison with competing products.

How much can you sell the product for? Are the products likely to sell? Checking out existing products will answer these crucial questions. Use the Amazon Bestsellers list as a reference point to identify your star products. A product rank under rank 1000 in a fairly large category means it is faring reasonably well, and can be considered for your inventory list.

Register to receive newsletter updates from reputed wholesalers or be a part of the mailing list of stores such Ikea and Walmart. They may send you special promos and offers or you can browse their website for popular or unique products. If you find a product that can be sourced really cheaply due to a limited period discount, try and order it in bulk and include it in your inventory. This way you can keep selling the product at a much higher price and rake in cool profits. Do not forget to take Amazon's fees into consideration while working out the price.

Private Label Products

Private label products are sold under your own brand name. You can source products in bulk directly from the manufacturer or wholesaler, and package the product with your label. You are therefore positioning the product as if it is being manufactured or supplied by your own firm.

Chapter 5: Create Membership Sites

Membership sites can help you rake in a good amount of passive income for a long time if you have a specific expertise that is sought after by plenty of people, especially expertise related to the virtual world. You may be an expert in creating smart-phone apps or copywriting or web designing or basically anything that people actively seek to learn. It can also be related to DIY and hobby based pursuits. How about language learning if you have mastery over a specific language or drone making if you know how to put together incredible drones?

At the onset, it is important to understand that membership sites need hard-work. You have to constantly keep updating, adding value, provide novel information and much more to keep your paid subscribers hooked. You must offer beyond exceptional value to retain your subscribers, which means it may not be a good option if you are just starting out in the online business world. Once you gain sufficient experience in a domain, you can consider launching your own membership site based business model. If you possess unique skills or knowledge which is in-demand, you can jump into it after doing some basic ground work. Since information is widely available everywhere, you must have something really unique to offer your audience if you expect them to pay for it.

Adding Membership Option To Existing Blogs

If your blog is already popular among a group of readers/users who are demanding more in-depth information from you, create a membership site and give them what they are looking for. For instance, if you run a blog that gives people ideas about what topics they can blog about or blog niche ideas and your audience suggests that you also include comprehensive keywords/keyword research reports for different niches, you can charge a premium membership fee for the detailed information. If you already have a blog or website, you simply need to add a membership site plug-in to it.

Start With a Few Complimentary Slots

Start by giving out the first few slots for free to build some response and reviews for your membership based site. The most positive and active folks on your mailing list, who are always adding value in the form of suggestions or discussions, can be considered for the giveaway. You can also consider giving away the first few slots at a discounted price with a coupon mailed to your loyal subscribers.

You may have a set of people who are regularly commenting on your blog posts or social media, while also contributing meaningfully to the discussions and helping other members. Make them your evangelists. Make them feel privileged by offering them free membership, and let them spread the word about your membership site.

Focus on Creating A Loyal Community

Membership sites are as much about a supportive and loyal community feel as they are about power packed information. The information will pretty much fade away over a period of time, however the relationship you build with your customers and the loyalty you inspire in them by adding value to their lives is what will keep them from leaving. Membership sites are all about creating a dedicated community of users where people support each other, resolve each other's queries and offer valuable guidance. Build a passionate following on the social media, and create a learning forum where members can swap ideas and solve other's issues. Ensure that you are prompt in your response when subscribers mail you with an issue.

Always ask for feedback from active subscribers. What aspects of the topic do they want to know more about? What other tools and software they need to optimize their results? What are the most common issues they come across while doing what you teach them to? Opinion polls are a great way to indentify the general sentiment related to various topics. You can build on topics that have been well-accepted and drop the ones that do not add much value.

You need to know exactly what your customers are looking for to hand it to them on a platter. Unscreen is a handy tool for monitoring and analyzing your audience activity. It lets you know which content type is generating optimal traction so you can create more of those.

Create High Quality Webminars

Tutorials and guides are much sought after in today's information packed digital world. People are looking for easier ways to perform multiple tasks. And what better to train people than to create high quality, interactive and information rich real time or pre recorded videos. One of the biggest advantages of these videos is that they can be accessed by followers across the world according to their convenience. Ask questions, conduct polls and stimulate discussions to inspire greater user interactivity. This will keep your audience glued from start to finish.

Use high quality and evocative visuals to make the matter more interesting and digestible. Visuals can be creatively weaved into the narrative to explain tricky concepts. You need to have a rough draft of how your presentation will flow, even if you aim to keep it more spontaneous. Create a rough table of topics, which you can elaborate on during the course of the webinar. If you are catering to a more global audience, use more universally accepted words, gestures and ideas.

Organize Your Information Efficiently

Once your site grows, you need to organize it efficiently to foster better navigation and access to information for new members. Guide your members through the maze of information by putting it all together in an orderly manner. If you find that new or existing users are asking you the same questions over and over on the social media or email, you can put together a handy Q & A page for newbies. Alternatively, have an introduction or 'begin here' page in place, where you can make new members feel less overwhelmed by all the information and guide them about navigating the available information in a step-by-step manner. Keep updating this section regularly.

Include a 'blast from the past' or 'refresher' section where you can re-post popular older blogs that members might have missed or link to those posts that are currently relevant.

Record A Friendly Welcome Video

One of the best ways to establish a warm rapport with your customers, and inspire their trust and loyalty is to record a cheery greeting video. It can be anything from a demonstration of how the site works or a story or a gentle reminder of the dos and donts. You can tell them how they can make optimal utilization of your services or how they can contact you should they stumble upon some issues or inspiring experiences of existing members.

Bring In The Influencers

You can offer free subscriptions to authoritative figures in your industry and ask them to leave behind genuine reviews about the site. People are likelier to take their unbiased report seriously, and give your site a look through. Since influencers have a fairly large follower base, your site will enjoy a wide reach among potential subscribers.

Create Group Events

Group events and challenges are a great way to engage existing members and keep them hooked. Motivate them and help them stay on track. It can be anything small like a challenge that helps subscribers attain a specific goal. For instance, if you run a membership site for writers who aspire to fulfill their writing goals, create a challenge video that encourages subscribers to complete a goal for the week. The buzz of working as a group/community can be wonderfully motivating, and creates a strong, positive vibe. You can also have other events, group challenges (where members compete with each other), courses and similar activities frequently to keep your subscribers on their toes.

Conclusion

The topics we covered are just a few of the most popular and more importantly, they are proven to be the most successful ways of making money passively. Whether you prefer to earn a passive income by selling photos or e-books or you are the type to get out and become a venture capitalist, what you need to remember is to keep your goal in the forefront of your mind. There will be trials and tribulations no matter what you choose. Stay focused, keep positive and you can most certainly find the niche that best fits your lifestyle.

I hope this book was able to help you to find a way to earn a passive income successfully and without having to go out and find a part-time job.

The next step is to test out a few of the tips and tricks to find the ones you like most for the type of passive income that will work best for you. The key component is to really take some time to consider where your passion lies because earning a passive income is about doing something you enjoy while making money passively...possibly even while you sleep!

www.ingramcontent.com/pod-product-compliance
Lightning Source LLC
Chambersburg PA
CBHW072208060526
44654CB00047B/1469